INCOMPARABLE

INCOMPARABLE

50 Days with JESUS

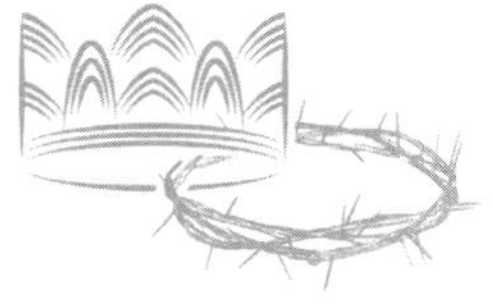

NANCY DEMOSS
WOLGEMUTH

MOODY PUBLISHERS
CHICAGO

This book is based on the *Revive Our Hearts* podcast series *The Incomparable Christ,* taught by Nancy DeMoss Wolgemuth.

All emphasis in Scripture quotations has been added by the author.

Published in association with the literary agency of Wolgemuth & Wilson.

Edited by Anne Christian Buchanan
Cover design: Brittany Schrock
Interior design: Erik M. Peterson
Author photo credit: Claire Thomas

ISBN: 978-0-8024-2953-7

Originally delivered by fleets of horse-drawn wagons, the affordable paperbacks from D. L. Moody's publishing house resourced the church and served everyday people. Now, after more than 125 years of publishing and ministry, Moody Publishers' mission remains the same—even if our delivery systems have changed a bit. For more information on other books (and resources) created from a biblical perspective, go to www.moodypublishers.com or write to:

Moody Publishers
820 N. LaSalle Boulevard
Chicago, IL 60610

1 3 5 7 9 10 8 6 4 2

Printed in China

No mortal can with Him compare
Among the sons of men;
Fairer is He than all the fair
That fill the heavenly train.
—Samuel Stennett (1727–1795)[1]

I beseech thee come, warm thy heart at this blessed fire!
O come, and smell the precious ointments of Jesus Christ!
O come, and sit under his shadow with great delight!
—Isaac Ambrose (1604–1664)[2]

And we all, with unveiled face,
beholding the glory of the Lord,
are being transformed into the same image
from one degree of glory to another.
—2 Corinthians 3:18 esv

Contents

Part Three: The Seven Last Words of Christ

Part Four: Now and Forever with Christ

Introduction

He asked his disciples, "Who do people say that I am?" . . .
"But you," he asked them, "who do you say that I am?"
—MARK 8:27, 29

Everyone has an opinion about Jesus. That became clear when Jesus Himself, while here on the earth, asked His closest followers what they had heard the crowds say about Him. They came up with an assortment of answers, just as people do today. Many nonbelievers will grant that Jesus was a good man, a wise philosopher, a moral example, a great teacher. Others, of course, insist He was a fraud, a fanatic. Some believe His words and influence are a menace to modern society. The majority, it seems, just clump Him together with various characters identified by history and tradition as founders of our world's religions.

"But you," Jesus said to His disciples, asking an even more pointed, more personal question, "Who do *you* say that I am?" That's what He really wanted to hear.

It's a question every one of us must eventually answer: "Who do you say Jesus is?" There is simply no escaping it. And whatever your answer, it carries serious implications for your life and future. So it needs to be based on more than mere conjecture or common knowledge. It needs to contain more than just Christian-sounding vocabulary.

Your answer needs to be based in truth. Truth that has been revealed to us. Truth that has stood the test of time and hate and derision and all the troubles endured by humankind, yet has continued to point to only one reasonable conclusion: Jesus is *incomparable*.

There is no one else like Him.

He alone is God in flesh. He alone died for the sins of the world. He alone was resurrected from the dead, never to die again.

It's a question every one of us must eventually answer: "Who do you say Jesus is?" There is simply no escaping it.

More personally, Jesus alone is able to save us from the sentence of death we rightly deserve. He alone is able to sanctify us, to change us, to make us holy and blameless before God. He alone is able to satisfy our thirsty souls, to give us rest and strengthen us when we grow weary of striving. And He alone, far from leaving us to struggle with our inability to please the Father, eternally lives to help us. To empower us. To defend us from the attacks and accusations that war against our souls, threaten our families, stunt our progress, and confuse our decisions.

Jesus is still here. And Jesus is still able.

Because Jesus is incomparable.

"Nobody else possesses his qualifications," wrote theologian John Stott. "We may talk about Alexander the Great, Charles the Great and Napoleon the Great, but not Jesus the Great. He is not the Great—he is the Only."[3]

With that in mind I invite you to join me on a journey to rediscover (or to discover for the first time) the power of this truth. We'll look together at the events of His earthly life—His birth, His childhood, His baptism, His temptation, and more. We'll ponder His deity; His humanity; His teaching, humility, and prayer life, and why all of it—why everything about Him—matters so dearly to each one of us. And we'll focus especially on the reasons He was put on trial, the purpose of His crucifixion, the significance of His seven final words from the cross, and the difference He has made for us by rising from the grave, returning to His Father, and continuing to minister to us from heaven while we await His second appearing.

I want you, when we're done, to be able to know exactly who Jesus is—who *you* say Jesus is—because of who the Word says Jesus is.

* * *

Like many other believers, each year I welcome the weeks leading up to Easter as an opportunity to pay even more focused, deliberate attention to who Jesus is and why He came to earth. During this season I often select a different book on the life and work of Christ to read and meditate on in my daily quiet times.

One of my all-time favorites is called *The Incomparable Christ,* written by a twentieth-century New Zealander, prolific author, and missionary statesman named J. Oswald Sanders. The insight I gleaned from reading his wonderful book inspired one of my teaching series some years ago and ultimately the book you're reading now. In fact, the table of contents for the book you're holding in your hand reflects the structure of Sanders' classic treasure.[4]

The fifty readings in this book can be used as a devotional companion during the six weeks leading up to Resurrection Sunday (Easter) and then in the week following. *Fifty days with Jesus.*

I make no apologies for these connections to another author's work. In fact, I hope that by drawing on the rich influence Sanders' writing has had in my life, I can encourage you to gaze upon the timeless beauty of Jesus.

If you happen to be reading this book in the early part of the year, may I suggest that you consider using it as a preparation guide for Easter? It's arranged in fifty readings—*fifty days* with Jesus—meaning you could use it as a devotional companion during the six weeks leading up to Resurrection Sunday and then in the week following Easter. (This will work if you count back six weeks from Easter Day and begin on that Sunday.)

But this book is certainly not limited to that use or that time frame. I hope it will draw you closer to Him at whatever time of year and whatever pace you choose to read it.

Because while learning more about Jesus is always valuable and important, both at Easter and all the time, our real reason for needing to know Him is to love Him, worship Him, trust Him, and obey Him, as well as to make Him known to others, spreading "the fragrance of the knowledge of him everywhere" (2 Cor. 2:14 ESV).

One thing is for sure: the more you know Him, the more you will come to find that He is indeed . . .

Incomparable.

Part One

THE PERSON OF CHRIST

I wish I could describe Him to you, but He's indescribable. . . .
He's incomprehensible. He's invincible. He's irresistible.
I'm trying to tell you, the heavens of heaven
cannot contain Him,
let alone a man explain Him.

—S. M. LOCKRIDGE[5]

Day 1

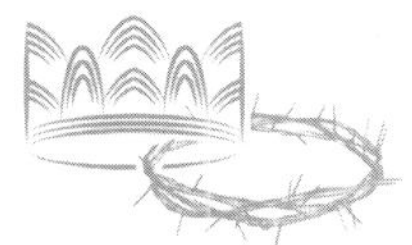

Somebody's Perfect

The Moral Perfection of Christ

"He has done everything well."
—MARK 7:37

Where to begin? In starting a book on Jesus, the options are truly unlimited. We could start before time, where He has existed for eternity—the uncreated Creator. We could start at a manger in Bethlehem, where He who made the universe condescended to inhabit planet Earth. We could start with the events leading up to what we now know as Easter, where His purpose in coming here came to full fruition and where we humans were given the inexpressible hope of living forever. With Him.

I believe we do well, however, right here at the beginning, to simply stand back and try to take in the overall reality of Jesus. His utter beauty. His true perfection.

He is altogether ideal.

This statement stands out most vividly to us when we consider how far short we fall of being ideal ourselves. We don't have it together *physically.* We don't have it together *spiritually.* We don't have it together *morally*. Hardworking and well-meaning as we may be, we are still sinners—repeat offenders desperately in need of a Savior.

We *wish* it weren't so. We *try* not to be. We feel the inner urge to do more and be more. To be different. To be better. Yet we consistently come up short, as does everyone else. People can be strong in certain areas, perhaps in several areas. We're even strong in a few ourselves. But none of us is strong in *everything*. We each possess our weak areas.

Stop and wonder, then, that Jesus has *no* weak areas. He is perfect in every way.

The writers who prophesied about Him in the Old Testament saw Him as "fairer than the sons of men" (Ps. 45:2 NKJV). Israel's Messiah, as envisioned in their minds under the inspiration of God's Spirit, was to be a man of perfection, surpassing all other humans.

But then to actually *meet* Him when He came, to spend time with Him, and to realize He truly was perfection at every turn, that you could find nothing at which He didn't excel . . . what an *incomparable* experience.

He is not merely good;
He is perfect.
He is not
merely enough;
He is everything.

This is not to say that Jesus struck everyone He met as being physically perfect. We have no New Testament evidence that He was the equivalent of a male model in His day, though as a carpenter He was surely fit. The prophet Isaiah had even stated that the coming Messiah

> didn't have an impressive form
> or majesty that we should look at him,
> no appearance that we should desire him. (Isa. 53:2)

Yet people did desire Jesus. They followed Him without question because no matter what His appearance, His beauty was unmistakable. He possessed every grace, every virtue, in perfect tension and balance. Not one of them was missing. Think of that. We've never seen what sheer perfection looks like in a person. Perfect symmetry between the inner and the outer. Perfect alignment of heart and character. It's almost impossible to envision such perfection. But there it is in Jesus.

He is not merely good; *He is perfect.*

He is not merely enough; *He is everything.*

He also kept the law of God perfectly. And let's be sure we're clear on what this means. Not only did He avoid committing even a single sin—an accomplishment that to our minds, knowing our struggles, is remarkable enough—but the perfection of Jesus went beyond mere sin avoidance. He actively lived the whole standard of God's law. None of it was for show. Everything He said and did was said and done with complete purity of motive. He fulfilled the law's mandate every moment of every day and went beyond that to fulfill the *spirit* behind the law.

I think of that memorable verse in Micah 6:

> He has told you, O man, what is good;
> and what does the LORD require of you
> but to do justice, and to love kindness,
> and to walk humbly with your God? (v. 8 ESV)

That's a solid summary of what God's law requires of us: perfect fairness and perfect love, delivered in perfect humility. That's precisely what Jesus did every second of His earthly life—and He did it perfectly. People could be overheard saying, "He has done all things well" (Mark 7:37). They couldn't help but notice.

So let us, too, pause to wonder at the perfection of Jesus.

He is not merely good; *He is perfect.*

He is not merely enough; *He is everything.*

He is not merely our Savior and Lord; *He is our one priceless treasure.*

We have in Him the most beautiful thing in all the world, the most desirable of all possessions—the most wonderful relationship a human being could ever possibly hope to have with anyone.

When we have Jesus, we have all we really need for time and eternity.

John Flavel, a Puritan pastor from the 1600s, in a sermon titled "Christ Altogether Lovely," asked his listeners to "cast your eyes among all created things, survey the universe."

> You will observe strength in one, beauty in a second, faithfulness in a third, wisdom in a fourth; but you shall find none excelling in them all as Christ does. Bread has one quality, water another, clothing another, medicine another; but none has them all in itself as Christ does. He is bread to the hungry, water to the thirsty, a garment to the naked, healing to the wounded; and whatever a soul can desire is found in him.[6]

Look anywhere else to find perfection, and you will never find it. Look to any other person as a model of flawless loveliness, and you will inevitably be disappointed. Look to anything or anybody—your spouse, your home, your job, yourself—to provide unmitigated satisfaction, and while you may see a number of impressive, desirable qualities there, you'll also see deficiencies that remind you they can never be everything you'll ever need.

But look to Jesus, and He will exceed your highest hopes.

Look to Jesus, and He will surpass your expectations.

Look to Jesus, and you will find yourself in the presence of utter perfection.

Is Christ your most precious treasure? What are some of the qualities you value most in Him?

How could a greater focus on the perfection of Jesus temper your disappointment with others? With yourself?

Oh Father, words fail to express the wonder of who Jesus is. He is lovely, He is good. He is perfect in every way. I don't have to look anywhere else, pursuing other things and other people, in hopes of being satisfied. In Him I have all that I need. May my life reflect His beauty to a world that desperately needs to see Your glory and grace.

AMEN.

Day 2

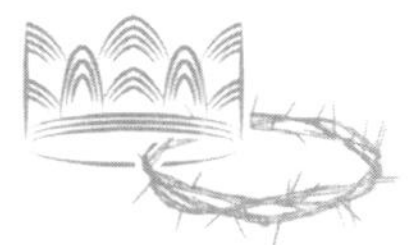

Ahead of Time

The Preexistence of Christ

He is before all things
and by him all things hold together.
—COLOSSIANS 1:17

My reading pile almost always includes at least one biography. I've loved these life stories since I was a girl and have quite the collection in my library. Most of the biographies I pick up feature a person I already know a little something about, whether it's a Christian missionary, a historical figure, a public servant, or just an individual who's accomplished something noteworthy.

But the part of most people's story that's usually less familiar to me is their backstory: where they came from, their family of origin, the circumstances surrounding their birth, and the bearing all of that had on the direction their life would take.

Jesus, though, breaks the mold on the biography model. For all the fuss we make about His birthday every year (and we should!), the Christmas event is not where His backstory begins.

Jesus lived *before* He was born.

Pause and ponder how that statement makes Jesus incomparable. His existence didn't begin with His miraculous conception and His birth in a stable. In fact, the Christmas story itself hints at His prior existence. Long before anyone ever sang "O Little Town of Bethlehem" on Christmas Eve, the prophet Micah foretold that from this inconsequential city would come a "ruler over Israel." But though this Ruler would be *born* there, He wouldn't *come* from there, because

his origin is from antiquity,
from ancient times. (Micah 5:2)

For another hint, page even further back through the Old Testament to Genesis 17, which describes the covenant God made with Abraham. Then fast-forward to the gospel of John, where Jesus outraged His first-century Jewish opponents by saying, "Before Abraham was, I am" (John 8:58).

That's right. Not "I was"—*I am.* Jesus not only defies the restraints of chronology but also the constraints of grammar. That's why John the Baptist, who was born to Elizabeth six months before Jesus was born to Mary (see Luke 1:36), could declare that "the one coming *after* me ranks *ahead of* me, because he existed *before me*" (John 1:15). Wow.

Jesus existed before *everything,* actually. There was never a time when He did not exist in all His fullness.

So what do we know about His life before He came to this earth? While much of this is mystery, we know that He was "with God" and that He "*was* God" (John 1:1). He had a close, personal relationship with God, living "at the Father's side" (v. 18). He was eternally one and equal with the Father, and He possessed all the glory of the Father (17:5).

And what was He doing in eternity past? One thing we know is that He was actively at work. For inside the mystery that's revealed to us as the Trinity—God the Father, God the Son, God the Holy Spirit—Jesus was the uncreated Creator of everything that exists.

"All things were created through him," states John 1:3, "and apart from him not one thing was created that has been created." In his letter to the Colossians, the apostle Paul further quantifies what is meant by "all things":

Everything was created by him,
in heaven and on earth,
the visible and the invisible,
whether thrones or dominions

> or rulers or authorities—
> all things have been created through him and for him.
> (Col. 1:16)

But Jesus is more than the Creator. He didn't just fling the universe into existence and hope it survived the trip. He was, is, and remains the Sustainer of our world. He's had it all under control from the beginning, and He holds it all together today—"sustaining all things by his powerful word" (Heb. 1:3).

Proverbs 8 gives us another glimpse of the preexistent life of Jesus. This passage is a personified description of *wisdom*. And Jesus, we're told in Scripture, is Himself "the wisdom of God" (1 Cor. 1:24). These verses take on new wonder when we read them in that light:

> "I was there when he established the heavens,
> when he laid out the horizon on the surface of the ocean,
> when he placed the skies above,
> when the fountains of the ocean gushed out . . .
> when he laid out the foundations of the earth.
> I was a skilled craftsman beside him." (Prov. 8:27–30)

Don't you love that picture? When God created the world, Jesus was there—not as a passive spectator, but actively working with His Father—just as He was when God devised and set in motion the plan of salvation. And as they worked together, they did it with joy:

> "I was his delight every day,
> always rejoicing before him.
> I was rejoicing in his inhabited world,
> delighting in the children of Adam." (vv. 30–31)

Through all of eternity, Jesus was a joyful God. The Father and the Son took great delight in each other.

Through all of eternity, Jesus was a joyful God. The Father and the Son took great delight in each other. And Jesus was "always rejoicing" not only in the created world but in its beloved inhabitants, "the children of Adam" (Prov. 8:31)—the people He'd made to inhabit His created world.

You.

Me.

Us.

We are His delight.

This is our Jesus—the One who told His disciples that He loved them the way the Father loved Him (John 15:9). Why did He want them to know that? "So that my joy may be in you and your joy may be complete" (v. 11)—the joy He has known with His Father from before time began.

And when the eternally existent Son broke into time, sent by the Father on a divine mission, He came to make it possible for us to experience what He had enjoyed for all of eternity.

How can knowing about Jesus' delight in the earth and the people He created help you deal with the sadness we experience in our broken world?

What foretaste does the existence of Christ before time began give us of what eternity with Him will be like for those who believe in Him?

Lord Jesus, I worship You, the eternally preexistent God. Thank You for breaking the time-and-eternity barrier in coming to us, so we can experience with You the love and joy You experience with Your Father. You are forever incomparable.

AMEN.

Day 3

Full Body of Work

The Incarnation of Christ

The Word became flesh and dwelt among us.
—JOHN 1:14

We're amazed today if we get home from the grocery store and realize we didn't forget anything on our list. We're amazed by the last-minute comeback we saw in a championship game we were watching on television. We're amazed that a package we ordered online arrived two days ahead of its projected delivery date.

Yet we're barely amazed anymore that the Son of God was conceived in a human womb and born into this world as a human being. The story is so familiar that it's easy to forget how stunning it really is. So maybe we need to take a fresh look at what theologian Wayne Grudem calls "by far the most amazing miracle of the entire Bible"—more amazing than creation, more amazing even than the resurrection. In fact, Grudem writes, it "will remain for eternity the most profound miracle and the most profound mystery in all the universe."[7]

It's another reason why Jesus is *incomparable.*

So let's be amazed by it again.

We will never fully understand, of course, the divine thinking behind this event called the *incarnation.* (The word comes from a Latin term that means "to make into flesh; to become flesh.") Why would Jesus choose to take on our human weaknesses, frailties, and limitations? Imagine being omnipotent, all-powerful, yet requiring the parental care of a mother and father. Imagine being omniscient, all-knowing, yet needing to learn how to walk; being the eternal Word of God, yet needing to learn how to read. Imagine having created the oceans, yet being thirsty for water. Imagine having spoken the stars into place, yet lying down at night underneath them.

Why would Jesus do this? He'd dwelt in heavenly places, in celestial palaces. Why would He submit to being born in a borrowed cattle shed? He was the beloved Son of God. Why would He agree to becoming the rejected Son of Man?

These are just a few of the many imponderables connected to the incarnation. The apostle John described it this way: "The Word became flesh and dwelt among us" (John 1:14). The Greek word translated "dwelt" in that verse literally means "tabernacled." In other words, Jesus "pitched His tent" with us.

- The infinite became finite.
- The immortal became mortal.
- The Creator became a creature.

Think of the humility involved in this exchange. Jesus, the Son of God,

> emptied himself . . .
> taking on the likeness of humanity. (Phil. 2:7)

Why? Because whether we understand it fully or not (which we can't!), only by His humbling Himself to this degree could we be saved from our sins. There was no other way. "He had to be like his brothers and sisters in every way" or else there'd be no "atonement for the sins of the people" (Heb. 2:17).

We would like to think our need is not this drastic. We've become so accustomed to our sins—fighting them, excusing them, confessing them, trying not to think about them—that even though we may hate them, we've found a way to go on living around them. But this familiarity in our relationship with sin disguises the depths to which it has toxified our hearts. We have incurred God's holy wrath because of our sin. We can't clear away the guilt from our sin. The inevitable outcome is that every sinner must die and be forever separated from God, from anything good, from anything else but the punishment we rightly deserve.

Except for the incarnation. That's the one and only game changer.

Jesus took on "flesh and blood," sharing in our human experience, "so that through his death he might destroy the one holding the power of death—that is, the devil—and free those who were held in slavery all their lives to the fear of death" (Heb. 2:14–15). That is, all of us.

The incarnation of Jesus is not just an ancient event that happened more than two thousand years ago. This wonder of wonders is very much a present-tense reality.

And that's the *why* of the incarnation, plain and simple. Amazing and sacrificial: "Christ Jesus came into the world to save sinners" (1 Tim. 1:15). To put it into language that rolls easily from memory, "God so loved the world, that he gave his only Son, that whoever believes in him should not perish but have eternal life" (John 3:16 ESV). We needed what only this gift could give us, and so God gave us the best that He had:

- Jesus, living our life without sinning
- Jesus, perfectly obeying the Father
- Jesus, dying our death in our place
- Jesus, paying our penalty for sin

And if that's not amazing, I don't know what is.

It's amazing enough that, as you hear it described again, I'm led to ask you: Do you sense His Spirit stirring you today in a way that perhaps you've never known before? Is He giving you desperation over your sinful condition? An understanding that Jesus has come to your rescue? A drawing of your heart to His own loving, gracious heart? Then run with me by faith into His forgiveness. Believe what He has said is true. And receive what He has said is yours.

There's no one else coming for us. We have Jesus, or we have nothing. We have this world with its constant disappointments and its occasional bursts of temporary peace and happiness, or we have eternal hope, God's saving grace, and the promise of life everlasting.

All because Jesus came and became one of us.

And oh, let's not forget that the incarnation of Jesus is not just an ancient event that happened more than two thousand years ago and that we celebrate each year on the twenty-fifth of December. This wonder of wonders is very much a present-tense reality. The God who became flesh, who came to dwell among us, who was crucified, buried, rose from the dead, and ascended to heaven, is seated today in His glorified human body at the right hand of the Father. He is still the God-man, our Advocate, who lives to intercede for us before the throne of God.

Stand amazed.

What would be different in your life if there had been no incarnation, if Jesus had not come to earth in human form?

How can you guard against becoming complacent about Christ's saving work for you?

Thank You, Father, for the mystery and the miracle of what Jesus did when He put on human flesh and came to this earth to save us from our sins. His humility and sacrifice confront my pride. Where would we be—where would I be—without Him? I'm amazed—and I praise you!

AMEN.

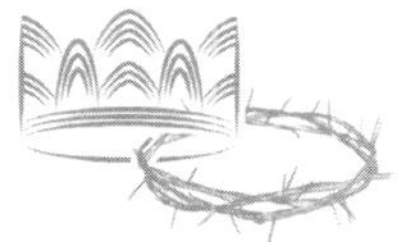

Day 4

Growing Up Jesus

The Childhood of Christ

The boy grew up and became strong, filled with wisdom, and God's grace was on him.

—LUKE 2:40

Within a century or two of Jesus' time on earth, speculation about what took place during His childhood years found its way into apocryphal accounts such as *The Infancy Gospel of Thomas*. You may have heard or read some of these fantastical stories about the young Jesus making clay birds that really flew, parting the waters of a brook in His boyhood village, or criticizing His schoolteachers for not knowing what they were talking about.[8]

Fascinating, right? Except none of these stories is true. Our only reliable source on the childhood activity of Jesus is what's told to us in Scripture. And perhaps what's most telling in this regard, as we scour the Bible for information, is that we're told almost nothing.

Jesus' childhood, like anyone's, was simply a childhood. Routine. Unspectacular.

Yet perhaps this tells us everything.

Because if anyone else had devised a story as inconceivable as the incarnation—a god coming to earth—it would never have included just an ordinary childhood, so unremarkable that it came with barely a mention in the historical recounting of His deeds. A god in the Greek sense of the word wouldn't have been given a childhood at all. Members of their mythological pantheon were assumed to arrive fully formed as adults. No childhood necessary, none desired. Having their legends diluted with images of childhood weakness, neediness, helplessness, dependence just wouldn't do.

Yet Jesus was so not that kind of god. His incarnation *for* us required identification *with* us, even down to His becoming a child. Part of what made this whole plan so ingeniously effective is that He restricted for a time the full use and expression of His divine capabilities so that He, like us, could experience all the normal developmental stages of childhood: the physical part, the intellectual part, the social part, the psychological part. All the parts. He didn't leapfrog from age three to age ten, for example, skipping the stages He didn't like, for the simple reason that we can't skip the stages we don't like. Instead He grew slowly, gradually, daily, incrementally, from one season to the next. The same way we do.

Jesus grew like us.

There's powerful importance in that—and purpose.

For though the Bible indeed says very little about His childhood, the clues it does give us about His family and growing-up years indicate a plan that perfectly prepared Him as a child for His incomparable mission and ministry as an adult.

Jesus grew slowly, gradually, daily, incrementally, from one season to the next. The same way we do.

He was born, for instance, to parents who were devout and godly, who lived "according to the law of the Lord" (Luke 2:39) and were faithful in worship (vv. 41–42). What better way for Jesus to learn the Scriptures and to develop reverence for God and His Word than to grow up in a home where God's ways were both lived and taught?

And yes, the things He learned as a boy were things He'd known for all eternity as the Son of God. But the *incarnated* Jesus learned about His heavenly Father the same way other kids learn about Him—a little bit at a time, building the foundation for a lifetime. And He did that in the home of earthly parents whose lives centered around the living God.

Jesus' childhood was not trouble free. His family was not spared the challenges of life in a fallen world. Jesus' mother, of course, had gotten pregnant with Him under circumstances not easily explained, so no doubt He grew up acquainted with looks and whispers, gossip and suspicion. Due to a government mandate, His mother had been forced to give birth seventy-five miles away from home in an inhospitable environment. Before he turned two, His life was threatened by a jealous king, and His parents had to flee hundreds of miles away to Egypt. And once the danger was past, the family returned to the small town of Nazareth, where Jesus grew up. No one expected much from anybody who came from there (John 1:46).

But even these adverse circumstances gave Jesus skills He'd need for later—how to handle being misunderstood, for instance, how to weather people's disapproval. All of this was part of God's early training ground for His Son on earth.

Jesus also grew up poor. We deduce this fact from the offering His parents brought to the temple for His dedication as a baby and for Mary's rite of purification following childbirth. The couple's choice of two common birds (Luke 2:24) reveals they didn't have "sufficient means" for a costlier, more presentable gift (Lev. 12:8).

If we didn't know the story, we might naturally expect that such a special child would be brought up in a family of wealth and name and position. How much more appropriate, however, that He wasn't. How fitting that "though he was rich, for your sake he became poor, so that by his poverty you might become rich" (2 Cor. 8:9).

What humility! Jesus was human like any other child. A son. A big brother. He *grew*, as we all must, from infancy, through childhood, to adulthood. But the Bible mentions another important detail about His story.

"The boy grew up," we're told in Luke's gospel, "and God's grace was on him" (2:40). Jesus grew up dependent on the favor of God. Contrary to *The Infancy Gospel of Thomas*, Jesus did not use His supernatural power as God to make birds or destroy His enemies. He laid aside that power. He grew as we have to grow. And He did so in reliance on the grace of God.

In ways we'll never fully understand, Jesus needed those years of childhood discovery—the obscurity of those slow-moving, simple, growing-up years—to learn that the one thing He needed more than anything else in life was the blessing only His Father could give Him.

Whether we realize it or not, we are all dependent—as are our children—on the care and keeping of God's grace. No matter our circumstances (whether good or bad), no matter our parenting style (whether hovering or permissive), no matter our family background (whether strong or dysfunctional), we ultimately are protected and guided by God's hand. We may think we are self-reliant, but the truth is, as we grow through every season of our lives, we are totally dependent on Him—His plans, His help, His behind-the-scenes work, and His favor on our behalf.

What difference does it make to us that Jesus went through every stage of normal childhood development?

What does it mean to you to depend on God's grace and favor on your life? How have you experienced that grace?

Father, thank You for sending Jesus as a baby who grew up in this world as a child. Thank You for His willingness to humble Himself, experience our lives, and share in our struggles. I acknowledge my need for Your favor and grace. Thank You that I can rely on it, as Jesus did, in every stage and season of life.

AMEN.

Day 5

Ever Increasing

The Youth of Christ

"Didn't you know that it was necessary for me to be in my Father's house?"
—LUKE 2:49

When did the boy Jesus become aware that He was the Son of God? We don't really know. But He certainly knew it by the time of a specific event recorded for us in Luke 2. I'm talking about the day—which stretched to two days, then to three—when He became so enthralled with the discussions taking place among the priests and teachers in the temple that He just couldn't tear Himself away from His "Father's house," even after His parents had headed home without Him.

By age twelve, Jesus knew exactly who He was.

Twelve today is middle school. Twelve today, by and large, is silly kids doing silly things. Sometimes they're still acting silly twelve years later or twenty years later. (Fifty years later?) But for Jewish boys during the days Jesus lived, the year leading up to their thirteenth birthday was when they prepared to officially become full members of the religious community of Judaism—"sons of the law" responsible to God for their own spiritual growth and development.

And Jesus embraced this passage to adulthood wholeheartedly.

This moment at the temple in Jerusalem is the only detailed portrait we have of Him before He emerged at the banks of the Jordan as a thirty-year-old man, ready to embark on His public ministry.

We have seen that as a boy Jesus "grew up" (Luke 2:40). Now we learn that as a teen He "*increased* in wisdom and stature, and in favor with God and with people" (v. 52).

The Greek word translated "increase" carries the idea of pioneers forging a pathway through the wilderness, cutting down trees in front of them that are blocking their way to a desired destination. It means to "beat" and "chop" and "hack" your way forward, undeterred by the denseness of the vines and the other obstacles in your way, exerting a strenuous effort to keep plowing ahead.[9]

Oh, that we would never stop *increasing,* as Jesus increased. Intentionally growing, deliberately advancing, refusing to stay idle or to settle for what we've already learned and obtained.

Increasing. That's the quality that Jesus was already modeling for us as a twelve-year-old. That's what we hear in the first spoken words attributed to Him in Scripture: "I must be in my Father's house" (Luke 2:49 ESV). Or "I must be about My Father's business" (NKJV).

Must! That word implies an increase of intensity, of determined purpose, that continued throughout His lifetime:

- "I *must* preach the good news of the kingdom of God" (Luke 4:43 ESV).
- "The Son of Man *must* suffer many things and be rejected" (Luke 9:22 ESV).
- "Everything written about me . . . *must* be fulfilled" (Luke 24:44).

But the "musts" in Jesus' life started at the temple. At age twelve. Or at least they blossomed there, building on the calling that had already been forming in Him as a child. From that point forward, nothing was optional to Him in His passionate pursuit of the Father's will. Nothing mattered more to Him than being completely surrendered, completely devoted, completely obedient. No distractions. No lazy diversions.

And how I love that we get to see this fire inside Him while He was still a young man. It's not as though He was defying His earthly parents. In fact, He stayed respectful and "obedient to them" as He continued to grow and mature in their home (Luke 2:51). But as a young teen He was already directing His attention toward His heavenly Father, increasing beyond His boyhood, looking ahead toward a responsible manhood and His redemptive ministry.

That's Jesus at twelve. That's the Jesus His mom and dad located after they'd scrambled back to Jerusalem from a full day's distance. (They hadn't noticed until nightfall that He was missing from the traveling party.) When they finally discovered Him there in the temple, He was "sitting among the teachers." And He was doing two important things—not only for twelve-year-olds, but for any-year-olds at any time in life. He was "listening . . . and asking questions" (Luke 2:46).

May we inspire the youth in our lives to find their greatest fascination not in typical teenage pursuits, but in developing a steady pattern of getting to know, really know, their heavenly Father.

Listening—that's an "increasing" type of activity. "Whoever listens to counsel is wise," says the writer of Proverbs 12:15. We don't learn and discern truth by hearing ourselves talk. We do it by listening to and processing what others are saying.

Asking questions. We also increase by being teachable. By wanting to know. By having a heart and hunger for growing in our understanding. Jesus queried the scholars in attendance and answered them back in ways that amazed them—not because He'd yet arrived at the fullness of His knowledge (not at twelve), but because He showed such an uncommon desire to learn.

May you and I be as eager, at whatever our age, to dig in to the Scriptures, to study them with others, to get our minds around the truths of God, and to be in our Father's house and service as Jesus showed Himself to be at twelve. And may we pray, challenge, and inspire the youth in our lives—whether our own children or others' children—to find their greatest fascination not in typical teenage pursuits, but in developing a steady pattern of getting to know, really know, their heavenly Father. Yes, even at twelve.

As Jesus did.

In what ways are you "increasing" in your understanding of the ways and the Word of God?

How might you be able to encourage the young people around you to pursue God during their formative years?

Father, the example of Jesus as a young man both convicts and inspires me. I pray that You would place a never-diminishing hunger in my heart to seek You and learn from You and know You. Make me alert to opportunities to pour into the lives of younger believers, that we may increase together in Your grace and grow into spiritual maturity.

AMEN.

Day 6

A Working Man

The Earthly Occupation of Christ

"Isn't this the carpenter, the son of Mary?"
—MARK 6:3

Eighteen years is a long time. A long wait. And isn't it remarkable, given the enormity of what Jesus came to do, that the Father's plan for His Son's relatively brief lifetime on earth included an *eighteen-year* gap between His childhood and His public ministry?

Think of that for a minute. The Son of God lived on this planet for thirty full years (Luke 3:23) before doing any of the work and wonders that marked the coming of His kingdom. It's only natural to wonder what He was waiting for. Was this an efficient use of His time? Why would He waste eighteen years in silent obscurity, apparently spending the bulk of that time working in His earthly father's construction business?

Answer: because work is not a waste of time.

And because God never wastes anything.

You may be at home with two preschoolers. You may be holding down a desk job or waiting tables (or doing one job right after the other!). Your plans for the afternoon may involve folding the laundry, carpooling kids from school to swim lessons and play practice, or answering calls in an order fulfillment center. But no matter what your job description, no matter how insignificant or menial your daily tasks may seem, that work is noble and sacred when it is done for the glory of God.

If that's not true, how do you explain Jesus working eighteen years as a carpenter? Would He have done it if He saw no purpose in it? Jesus was no less engaged in doing His Father's will—being "about [His] Father's business" (Luke 2:49 NKJV)—during the eighteen years from age twelve to age thirty than He was during the three years we call His ministry years.

"The carpenter"—that's how Jesus was known for the larger part of His life. The term may have been intended more as a put-down than a compliment. Elsewhere in Scripture, there are many lofty titles for Jesus—Son of God, Prince of Peace, Lord of glory. But during those young-adult years of His life, Jesus was referred to simply as "the carpenter" or "the carpenter's son."

Jesus placed Himself under the burden of hard work—the same burden as *our* hard work—and transformed it into a daily offering of obedience.

He didn't have any formal theological training or professional credentials on His resume. He was a common working man. Someone who worked with His hands. Someone whose business was building things. Someone whose clothes got sweaty and dirty by the end of the day. (I wonder what the angels must have thought as they looked on!)

But Jesus' example of humble earthly work only adds to what makes Him *incomparable.*

Jesus didn't choose to just hang out until it was time to begin His public ministry; He wasn't idle or slothful. He glorified His heavenly Father by working diligently with His hands through all those years—perhaps supporting His mother and other family members after Joseph died.

Work, contrary to what many assume, is not a curse from the fall. When God placed Adam in the garden of Eden—before sin ever entered the equation—the Lord gave him the assignment "to work it and watch over it" (Gen. 2:15).

From the beginning, work has been meant as a blessing. Work is good. Work is from God—and not just preaching and teaching work. Menial work is also included. Routine work. Hard work. Grunt work. The kind of work *all* of us do—because all of us have elements of our daily responsibilities that are not easy or inherently fulfilling, but that need to be done.

In our culture we tend to place greater significance on high-paying, high-visibility types of work. We measure the value of what we do in terms of scope, impressiveness, and impact. But Jesus' example shows that God rewards diligence, faithfulness, and humble service.

J. Oswald Sanders pointed out, "If it was not beneath the Son of God to work as an artisan, then surely it is beneath none of His children."[10] I love seeing Jesus in that light, demonstrating to us that all work done well and productively—and done for God's glory—is noble work, beautiful work, sacred work, spiritual work. Scripture makes this point explicitly:

- "Whatever you do, in word or in deed, do everything in the name of the Lord Jesus, giving thanks to God the Father through him" (Col. 3:17).
- "Whatever you do, do it from the heart, as something done for the Lord" (Col. 3:23).
- "Whatever you do, do everything for the glory of God" (1 Cor. 10:31).
- "Whatever you do"—whatever *you do*—can be done to "serve the Lord Christ" (Col. 3:24).

Jesus worked in this way for eighteen years of His life—another important way He shared in our humanity. Because while work was indeed a part of life prior to the fall, we now live with certain aspects of work that sting with suffering as a direct consequence of the fall. Genesis 3 predicted that, as a result of the first humans' sin, work would now be tedious and "painful" (v. 17), a constant struggle against opposition and obstacles, against "thorns and thistles" (v. 18). Work would be wearying and fatiguing, done by "the sweat of [our] brow" (v. 19).

Most of us can relate to work that feels like that—backbreaking, mind-numbing labor. And Jesus does too. By experiencing the tedium and exertions of rigorous labor, Jesus bore the consequence of sin placed upon the human race.

He could've spent those eighteen years doing nothing, living in limbo, waiting for the real work of ministry to begin. Instead He placed Himself under the burden of hard work—the same burden as *our* hard work—and transformed it into a daily offering of obedience. He toiled for the glory of God while working with His hands, just as He later would labor for the glory of God while preaching "good news to the poor," proclaiming "release to the captives," bringing "recovery of sight to the blind," and setting "free the oppressed" (Luke 4:18).

It was all one seamless block of work to Him. "My Father is still working," He said, "and I am working also" (John 5:17).

And we are working also. Working with and for our Father. Every day.

What kinds of work do you find difficult to carry out faithfully and joyfully?

How does reflecting on Jesus' work life shape your perspective on the ordinary, routine, or obscure tasks your work requires?

Father, thank You for the work You've given me to do. I receive it as a gift, an opportunity to serve You and others and to fulfill Your purpose for me in this season of life. When my work is hard, when it's unpleasant, when it feels like more than I can do, remind me that You understand my pain and impatience and that I can do all things through You.

AMEN.

Day 7

All for One

The Singleness of Christ

"I delight to do your will, my God,
and your instruction is deep within me."
—PSALM 40:8

How often do we look at Jesus only through our Sunday school glasses? We see Him in the framed art, the stained-glass windows. We know Him through the snippets of His life recounted in the Gospels. But to view Him from such a historical distance is to discount the fact that He encountered the same rhythms and rigors of life as we do. He is not merely the sum of His most memorable moments. He lived here on earth as a real man.

Jesus lived a daily life. Midmornings. Afternoons. Late nights. All of it.

And He lived all of it unmarried.

Yes, Jesus was a single man. He had friends, of course, but not the companionship of a wife. He thoroughly enjoyed being with children, but He didn't have any kids of His own at home to love and teach and spend time with.

We've always known this fact about Him, of course, but we tend not to pay a lot of attention to it. We don't often delve into how His single status contributed to the life He lived. We just think that, well, He was God, so He didn't need a wife. He was God, so He didn't need His own children.

But Jesus was also a man. And as a man He felt all the normal human desires we feel. He lived His young-adult years experiencing the natural longings of anyone His age, and He continued to experience them as He neared thirty and beyond. He attended friends' weddings. He went to parties and dinners. He interacted with other men who were husbands and fathers. We can only assume that the thought of a family life might have appealed to Him, even though He was here on a unique mission.

So we should not be surprised when the Bible tells us that Jesus was "tempted in every way as we are" (Heb. 4:15). Now, when we think of being "tempted," we may have in mind the inner struggle that takes place when we fight a desire to sin. Unlike us, however, Jesus had no sin in Him and therefore no *sinful desires* that had to be rejected. But He *was* tempted in terms of experiencing human (not sinful) *weakness* (which we see highlighted in Hebrews 4:15). He was able to be tempted through such normal desires as hunger, thirst, the threat of pain, and—as a single man—through natural human longings and feelings that were not the Father's will to be fulfilled.

The truth is, our hearts can never really be filled by another human being, by a different living situation, nor by any alternate scenario we may have envisioned for our future.

Again, our soft watercolor images don't do much to help us see this side of Jesus, but the panorama of Scripture gives us an unvarnished, realistic picture of His life. That means He dealt with the same kinds of normal human desires in His day that can come with being single in our day.

This realization should bring us hope and encouragement. Because all of us have longings. All of us have things we lack, things we want, even things we believe we legitimately need. And these things—marriage and family included—can consume our focus and attention, especially when we have to live without them. It's easy for us to make idols of our longings and use them to justify all kinds of unhealthy or even sinful thoughts and actions.

But Jesus never did this. He never gave natural desires the authority to become demands. He never used them as an excuse for making moral compromises or disobeying the Father in any way. So what did He do when He was bombarded by unmet longings?

He didn't suppress them. He didn't deny they existed. He simply trusted His needs to His Father. He found satisfaction in His Father's companionship. Rather than chafing at being single or at the physical, emotional, or relational sacrifices He was called upon to make, He embraced and delighted in His Father's will. That was enough for Him. It satisfied Him.

I think most of us know our relationship with the Father is supposed to be like that. His companionship is supposed to be as completely satisfying to us as Jesus found it to be. But sometimes we're lonely, and we want someone to be there. When we're carrying more than we feel we can manage on our own, we want to go home to someone who'll provide a listening ear, a caring heart, and wise input, the way everyone else (it seems) gets to do.

You can be single and feel that way (as I can attest, having been unmarried for the first fifty-seven years of my life). You can be widowed and feel that way (as my eighty-five-year-old mother knows so well, having been widowed since she was forty). And (as every person who's been married for more than a week knows) you can even be married and feel that way—because no one, not even a spouse, can fill our cavernous hearts and fulfill all our needs, real or perceived.

But realizing we have a Savior who has walked that path and understands that feeling can do a lot to help us handle it in healthy, godly ways. We have the incomparable Christ as a living example, assuring us that we can submit our unfulfilled longings to the Father. We can forfeit pleasures that are afforded to others. And we can tap into a revitalizing joy that lies before us (Heb. 12:2), even if we've hoped for our cup to be filled another way. Because the truth is, our hearts can never really be filled by another human being, by a different living situation, nor by any alternate scenario we may have envisioned for our future.

"Consider" Jesus, the Bible says, "so that you won't grow weary and give up" (Heb. 12:3). Consider how He lived His single life. Consider the mindset He brought to His mission: "I have come to do your will" (Heb. 10:9). Ask for His help to make that your mindset as well. And, regardless of what your present circumstances may be telling you, cling to the promise that in the end you will find, as Jesus did, that

- in God's will is "the path of life"
- in His "presence is abundant joy"
- in His "hand are eternal pleasures" (Ps. 16:11)

In what area of life are you currently feeling a sense of lack or loss or unfulfilled longing?

How can considering Jesus provide hope and grace to meet the deepest needs of your heart?

Father, as I sit here today, alone with You,
I thank You for the reminder that Jesus, in some
way, has felt everything I'm feeling, everything
I will ever feel. Thank You for surrounding and
filling me with Your love. Let Your love flow
through me to minister grace to others who are
feeling empty and needy.
AMEN.

Day 8

The Heavens Declare

The Baptism of Christ

"This is the way for us to fulfill all righteousness."
—MATTHEW 3:15

Easter Sunday, 1964, marked one of my earliest and most unforgettable memories. I was five when my childhood pastor, Earl Connors, baptized me that day, nearly a year after I first trusted Christ to save me. Before my baptism, the deacons of our little Baptist church had gathered to listen to my personal testimony and confirm that I was ready to take this momentous step.

Since that day I've attended many baptismal services, and I never get tired of them. Few experiences are so pure, so hopeful, so powerful as hearing and seeing that first gasp from someone surging up from the water—the look on their face, the freshness in their smile as they declare their loyalty to Christ and publicly express the change He's brought about in their repentant heart. "Raised from the dead," like Jesus from the grave, they rise now to "walk in newness of life" (Rom. 6:4).

Yet as beautiful as that picture is, as meaningful as it is to witness each of these ceremonies, I've never seen a baptism like Jesus' baptism. Except for those present on the banks of the Jordan River that day, nobody has. Because that baptism, like Jesus Himself, was truly *incomparable.*

For one thing, unlike us, Jesus had no sins to confess, no wickedness to repent of, no need for salvation from God's wrath. When He stepped into the baptismal waters, He was identifying with *our* need to be washed from our sins. When He joined with those who were streaming to the Jordan to be baptized by His cousin John, He was also fulfilling prophecy by being "numbered with the transgressors" (Isa. 53:12 ESV)—that's us!—so that we, by faith, could one day count *His* righteousness as *our* righteousness. In addition, He was reenacting a powerful ceremonial rite instituted long ago under the Old Testament law.

It's no coincidence, you see, that Jesus was thirty years old at the time of His baptism. According to the instructions given to Moses in Numbers 4, thirty was the age at which priests became "qualified" (v. 3) to perform the duties of their office. And before assuming those responsibilities, each priest underwent a special ritual established by God to symbolically set them apart for the work that lay before them.

Because of Jesus' ministry on our behalf, formally initiated at His baptism, we have been granted the gift of His Spirit along with the Father's blessing, assuring us that we are beloved sons and daughters with whom He is well-pleased.

Aaron, the brother of Moses, and Aaron's sons were the first ever to participate in this ceremony. Moses presented them to the Lord before the gathered congregation of God's people and "washed them with water" (Lev. 8:6) to cleanse and sanctify them. For Aaron, who had been designated as the high priest, God's instructions went further. After clothing his brother in priestly garments, Moses took oil and poured it on Aaron's head (v. 12).

All this water, all this pouring, did so much more than get these men wet. It signified their being drenched in God's holiness, consecrated, and anointed for service. And it set a precedent for the time, centuries later, when Jesus, God's appointed High Priest, would go into and rise up out of the waters of baptism. Holy, obedient, humble, and surrendered, He, too, would receive an anointing—an anointing like none other.

That moment as described in the Gospels was a powerful one. "The heavens suddenly opened" (Matt. 3:16). Then "a physical appearance like a dove" emerged from the skies, descending on Jesus (Luke 3:22), accompanied by the sound of an audible voice: "You are my beloved Son; with you I am well-pleased" (Mark 1:11). Peter would later describe this as the moment when "God anointed Jesus of Nazareth with the Holy Spirit and with power" (Acts 10:38).

No, we've never seen a baptism like that.

But think what this means, this opening of the heavens at Jesus' baptism.

Travel back with me to the day when Adam and Eve were driven from the garden of Eden, shut out by their own sin. The access to God's presence they'd once been privileged to enjoy was no longer within their reach. And this restriction applied not only to Adam and Eve but to every person who would ever live.

In fact, the underlying premise behind all the religions of the world is humankind's relentless attempts to regain access to God. Every religious pursuit apart from belief in Christ amounts to our best efforts to get heaven to open up, hoping all our work and effort will somehow please Him enough that He'll let us into His presence and give us a life that continues after death.

But when Jesus stood there praying after His baptism, "heaven opened" (Luke 3:21). Now, heaven had never been closed to Him. Due to His sinless nature and obedient life, He had never forfeited acceptance with God. But there at the Jordan, He received from above the anointing of the Holy Spirit and the spoken blessing of His heavenly Father. This is the point that launched Jesus into His earthly ministry—a mission that would open those same heavens to rebellious sinners by virtue of His righteousness.

This is why the first Christian martyr, Stephen, in the fleeting moments before his violent death, could say, "Look, I see the heavens opened and the Son of Man standing at the right hand of God!" (Acts 7:56).

It's why John the apostle, receiving his revelation in exile on the isle of Patmos, could look into heaven and see "an open door," hear a voice inviting him to "come up here," and observe the glory of a "throne in heaven" with God Himself "seated on it" (Rev. 4:1–2).

And—hallelujah!— it's why you and I are not stuck here on earth with nothing but this fallen world to look at and nothing but separation from God to look forward to for all eternity. The heavens are open to us, too, because Jesus has opened them for us.

"Come up here," He says, where the hard work of religion can never take us, but where His righteous work on our behalf has "torn open" the heavens (Mark 1:10) and torn down every barrier that restricts our access to the throne of God (15:38). Because of Jesus' ministry on our behalf, formally initiated at His baptism, we have been granted the gift of His Spirit along with the Father's blessing, assuring us that we are beloved sons and daughters with whom He is well-pleased.

See if that doesn't change the way you worship at the next baptism you see.

Have you been baptized as a follower of Jesus? If so, how does His baptism add fresh insight and significance to yours?

How would your life and outlook be different today if heaven remained closed, if Christ hadn't given you access to the Father?

Holy Father, I am moved by the way Jesus fulfilled all the requirements of righteousness at every turn, from beginning to end. Thank you that He has opened the way to You for every sinner who looks to Him. By His righteousness, not my own, I come to You, and I live today by faith in Him.

AMEN.

Day 9

Shared Victory

The Temptation of Christ

Since he himself has suffered when he was tempted,
he is able to help those who are tempted.
—HEBREWS 2:18

You've most likely never attempted (or succeeded at) a forty-day fast the way Jesus did. And it's certain you've never spent those forty days in a physical wilderness as He did, with wild animals surrounding and invading your camping space (Mark 1:13). But when considering the account of Jesus' temptation in Scripture, you may be surprised to discover you have a lot more in common with His experience than you'd thought.

First, have you noticed how often some of your most intense seasons of temptation have followed directly—"immediately" (Mark 1:12)—on the heels of an unusually thrilling moment? After a great victory or accomplishment? After a satisfying turn of events, perhaps at work or in your family's life? Rather than just an uncanny coincidence, that may well be a diabolical plan. Satan looks for every opportunity where he can catch us unaware or unprepared to face him in battle. He also knows we're rarely more vulnerable to his suggestions, more drawn toward ease, complacency, or pride, than when we're basking in the glow of a hard-won battle.

We see this borne out in Jesus' wilderness experience. He went there with the audible blessing of His Father still ringing in His heart—the affirmation that God was "well-pleased" with His "beloved Son" (Matt. 3:17). In the wake of that public pronouncement, Satan must have assumed Jesus was vulnerable to compromise. Know the feeling? The enemy uses similar tactics against us.

But notice, too, how Jesus defeated these advances. You might expect He would wage war by deploying the indestructible tools available only to the Son of God, overpowering the enemy by the sheer force of His divinity. Instead, the resources Jesus brought to the fight were the same ones available to you and me today as we deal with the devil's schemes and enticements to sin.

When facing temptation in the wilderness, Jesus relied on:

- *the Holy Spirit,* who had led Him there (Matt. 4:1)
- *prayer,* which He was already in the habit of employing (Luke 3:21)
- *the grace of God,* granted to Him in His humble acknowledgment of need
- *the Word of God,* bringing truth to bear on the enemy's lies

How reassuring to realize that we each have those weapons in our spiritual arsenal! Jesus overcame temptation the same way any of us can overcome temptation—by drawing on the resources every believer already possesses. And in so doing He thoroughly trounced the enemy.

When Satan challenged Jesus to "tell these stones to become bread" (Matt. 4:3)—to satisfy His hunger in His own way rather than waiting patiently for His Father's provision—Jesus refrained. Which means *Jesus won.*

When Satan dared Him to hurl Himself down from a death-defying height (v. 6) to prove God's promises were real (instead of believing God's promises regardless), Jesus said no—and *won again.*

Even when offered "all the kingdoms of the world and their splendor" (v. 8) without the pain or mess of dying on the cross, Jesus refused—*another win.*

Three up, three down. When coming up against Satan's temptation,

Jesus won every time. And He did it by tapping a supply line of defenses also offered to us.

So we should take heart when doing battle against our adversary. We are not on our own or at a loss. We step onto the battlefield armed with the same weapons as Jesus. The only difference is that we're not out there by ourselves trying to put them into practice. For Jesus Himself is there to aid us:

- "Since he himself has suffered when he was tempted, he is able to *help* those who are tempted" (Heb. 2:18).
- "Therefore, let us approach the throne of grace with boldness, so that we may receive mercy and find grace to *help* us in time of need" (Heb. 4:16).

This "help" provided us, according to the term used in the original Greek text for these verses, works like a rope or chain lashed around a boat, a sailing vessel, to keep it from falling apart. The noun form of this verb appears earlier in the New Testament to describe efforts made by the mariners on board Paul's ship when its voyage to Rome was interrupted by high winds and storm: "They used *ropes and tackle* and girded the ship" (Acts 27:17). These "helps" reinforced the boat so it could survive the pounding waves.

Jesus overcame temptation the same way any of us can overcome temptation—by drawing on the resources every believer already possesses.

With that in mind, picture Jesus coming out to where we're struggling, where the temptations seem to be battering us to death, where we're sure we'll go under at any minute and lose another fight against the evil one. Seeing us sinking, He wraps us in His mighty, sustaining power. He holds us together as the assaults against us intensify. We're never alone in our suffering because He's here to undergird us, to support us, to get us safely through.

He can do it because He's already done it, because He's been tempted and tried Himself, "yet without sin" (Heb. 4:15). He's confident we will emerge as victors because He knows all about the weapons available for fighting temptation. He's put them to the test and found them capable.

What more or better help could we need than the help Jesus gives?

When Jesus refused to yield to Satan's temptation in the wilderness, He served notice to all the powers in heaven and hell that He was the sovereign Lord and would not bow to Satan. There in the wilderness and later in the garden of Gethsemane, Christ dealt Satan one blow after another, foreshadowing that final, fatal blow at Calvary and the enemy's ultimate banishment at the end of the age.

Because Jesus overcame temptation, we can overcome temptation. And because of His victory over the tempter, one day we will be free from the tempter and from all temptation forever.

In what areas of your life are you most tempted to try to fight the battle alone rather than turning to Jesus for help?

Which of the resources available to you (and to Jesus) could you learn to trust more deeply and use more often in your battle against sin?

Father, You know the battles I face against my sin and my flesh. You know where I struggle and where I fail. How I need Your help—and how comforting and invigorating it is to know You are always here to offer it. To support me. To strengthen me. To hold my little ship together. I come to You today by Your grace, holding fast to the truth of Your Word, trusting You for victory!

AMEN.

Day 10

God in Flesh

The Deity of Christ

The entire fullness of God's nature dwells bodily in Christ.

—COLOSSIANS 2:9

Dan Brown's hit novel *The Da Vinci Code* has sold more than eighty million copies since its 2003 release, making it one of the most popular works of fiction in publishing history.[11] And fiction it is—both in the narrative sense and in some of the untruths it propagates. One of these is that the doctrine of Jesus' deity was contrived by church leaders three hundred years after His death in order to bolster their religious authority. "Until *that* moment in history," Brown writes, speaking in one of his character's voices, "Jesus was viewed by His followers as a mortal prophet . . . a great and powerful man, but a *man* nonetheless."[12]

Which is a problem if someone accepts this fiction as fact.

And many do just that.

Most people have no issue with Jesus being a historical reality, even a historical highlight, as long as He remains only a human. Jesus the *man,* they think, can be held at a safe distance. He can be appreciated for how His teaching and example both inspire and enlighten. Jesus the man is tolerable, manageable, quotable, and measurable.

Jesus as *God,* however, is different. If Jesus is God, then what we believe about Him is not just a matter of cultural relevance but of eternal significance.

Jesus as God holds us accountable. Jesus as God determines the course of our lives.

The conviction that Jesus is God goes back a lot further than the fourth century AD. Further even than Jesus' life on earth.

The prophet Isaiah, for example, writing seven hundred years before His birth, wrote that a "virgin shall conceive and bear a son, and shall call his name Immanuel" (Isa. 7:14 ESV), which means, "*God* is with us" (Matt 1:23).

Isaiah went on to tell more about this child who would be "born for us," on whose shoulders would ride the full power and command of divine government (Isa. 9:6). The given names of this coming child (in addition to Immanuel) make His divinity clear:

> Wonderful Counselor, Mighty God,
> Eternal Father, Prince of Peace. (v. 6)

But if the words of Old Testament prophecy sound too obscure to some, too mysterious to be regarded as evidence, the plain words of Jesus Himself should suffice. They contradict any claim that He was not considered divine during His lifetime. For Jesus directly affirmed His divinity, stating that "I and the Father are one" (John 10:30) and that "the one who has seen me has seen the Father" (John 14:9). In fact, it's upon this ground that Paul the apostle, in the years immediately following Christ's resurrection, declared Him "the image of the invisible God" (Col. 1:15) and stated that

> God was pleased to have
> all his fullness dwell in him. (Col. 1:19)

In His only Son. In Jesus the man, the Son of God.

Not merely *a* son of God, as some religions claim.

Not a *creation* of God, as others believe.

Jesus is God Himself. That's the truth—or else Christianity is false. There are many important implications of this reality. Here are just three of them:

1. Because Jesus is God, it is possible for us to know God—through Christ.

From earliest times, not even someone of the spiritual stature of Moses was allowed the privilege of actually seeing the God "who is invisible" (Heb. 11:27). People occasionally heard His voice; they could write down what He said. And in Exodus 33:19–23, Moses was allowed a brief glimpse of God's "glory" from the back. But no one had ever really "seen God" in His fullness until they saw Jesus. "The one and only Son, who is himself God and is at the Father's side—he has revealed him" (John 1:18).

Pause to take in the wording of that verse again. By looking at the Son, we see the Father—not merely because He is God's human representative, His ambassador to this earth, but because Jesus "is himself God." He is "the radiance of God's glory and the exact expression of his nature" (Heb. 1:3).

Jesus has not left us to wonder what the Father is like. Our Father is like what we see in His Son. Jesus Christ is how we know Him—and also how we draw near to Him.

2. Because Jesus is God, He has provided for us the one and only way to the Father.

The world thinks of Jesus as being one way to God among many. The idea is that we're free to pick and choose what seems best to us, but we can't claim our way is the only way. And, honestly, a defensible argument could be made for that position. Christianity could be just another alternative in a religiously pluralistic universe—if Jesus were not God.

But if it's true that sin has left an indelible stain on every human soul and that no one can stand before a holy God on the merits of his or her own righteousness, we need a righteousness that comes from somewhere else, from Someone as righteous as God. We need a God who can save us, not a religious system we can subscribe to.

The reason "there is salvation in no one else," in "no other name" but the name of Jesus (Acts 4:12), is that no one's good works can do what only God can do, through what Jesus has done. Because of who Jesus is. Because Jesus is God.

3. Because Jesus is God, He is to be worshiped, trusted, and obeyed as God.

What right does He have to demand our total worship and allegiance if He is only a man? But if He is God—or, I should say, because He is God—how can we legitimately worship anyone or anything else?

The founder of Christianity—Jesus Christ Himself—claims to be God. No one else needed to make the claim *for* Him. He made it on His own, and He has saved us as His own.

That's why none of us needs to despair that we must find God on our own.

Though Jesus certainly did become a human, what do we stand to lose by overemphasizing His humanity at the expense of His divinity?

What difference does it make in your relationship with Jesus to know that He is fully God?

I bow before You, "our great God and Savior, Jesus Christ" (Titus 2:13). Help me to identify and dethrone any idols, any false gods that I've allowed to take Your place in my heart. My worship, love, and obedience belong to You and You alone. I owe my life to You, to Your divine grace and Your saving power.

AMEN.

Day 11

Made Like Us

The Humanity of Christ

There is one God and one mediator between God and mankind, the man Christ Jesus.

—1 TIMOTHY 2:5

The cattle are lowing, the baby awakes.
But little Lord Jesus, no crying He makes.

It's a lovely song, a favorite Christmas lullaby. I'm glad we get to hear it and sing it every year. But I feel pretty sure that baby Jesus, away in that manger, made full use of His newborn lungs and did His share of crying. We've become so conditioned by the haloed artwork and the overly sentimentalized portrayals of Jesus as a baby, a child, and a man that I think we may have lost the real picture.

Jesus was a human being.

Yes, we've already referenced that as we explored the meaning of the incarnation. But I think it's worth taking another look, to consider more fully the implications of Jesus living as a human on earth.

He looked like us. He breathed in and out like us. He had a physical body just as we do.

His experiences on earth differed from ours only in that He was God (we're not God) and He had no sin (we, of course, have more sins than we wish to count). But in every other way Jesus was like *us*. When people saw Him in town, they didn't suspect He came from another species. When He sat down for a meal, He ate like everybody else in His part of the world. When He traveled from place to place,

He didn't fly around like Superman. He needed ten minutes to take a ten-minute walk.

He was human. His body could experience pain. His skin bruised when He was struck. His veins bled when He was cut. Further, he experienced physical limitations and weaknesses. He knew what it was to be weary, hungry, and thirsty.

And Jesus not only had a physical body, as we do. He also experienced human emotions. He had a human soul along with His human body—a full human makeup.

Again, the paintings depict Him, for the most part, without much animation or expression, looking mild to the point of mystical. But Jesus was hardly a dry-eyed, joyless, unfeeling robot. He "marveled," for example, at the faith of a Roman centurion (Matt. 8:10 ESV). He "felt compassion" for the "distressed and dejected" (Matt. 9:36). He was "glad" for those He loved who were growing into their faith (John 11:15). But He could also be "troubled in his spirit" (John 13:21), sometimes voicing His prayers with "loud cries and tears" (Heb. 5:7). At the tomb of His good friend, Lazarus, Jesus' first response was to weep (John 11:35).

All this is to say that in Jesus we see the glory of God's original design for us humans—a man truly bearing the Father's image, nature, and likeness. The kind of person you and I were created to be and would have been if our bodies and souls had not been tainted by sin.

There are those who fall into the trap of assuming the physical part of us is bad. We're susceptible to feeling shame or displeasure in our appearance—the parts we don't like, the problem areas we so often wrestle with. Yet the body was clearly of great value and importance to Jesus. Don't forget that He kept a human body after His death and resurrection. "Look at my hands and my feet," He said to His disciples when He appeared to them on that first Resurrection Day. "It is I myself! Touch me and see" (Luke 24:39).

The same applies to emotions. You may have grown up thinking that feelings are dangerous or unseemly and should be suppressed instead of being expressed, whether in public or in private. But Jesus, again, displayed a wide range of human emotion. So having feelings—or even displaying them honestly—is obviously not wrong. The issue is when our emotions are sinfully motivated or are the result of sinful desires. Or when we convey those feelings at the wrong time or place or let them lead us into sinful thoughts or behavior.

As a man, Jesus demonstrated the appropriate way to show human emotions. He felt perfectly free to express them, but in a balanced, wholesome, and godly way. His heart was moved by the things that move the heart of God. His emotions synced up with the truth. They reflected kingdom values, not petty personal likes, grudges, and preferences.

Jesus walked in our skin. He showed us what mankind, created in the image of God, was meant to be.

Jesus lived out this entirety of the human experience in a fallen world and culture, rubbing shoulders with fallen men and women, which means He had to deal with the same challenges we go through. He still embodied perfection, of course, but He had to maintain it in the midst of earth's imperfections.

And that's what makes His coming here as a human so remarkable. That's what should fill us with awe and worship. Jesus knew exactly what He would face when He came to this world, yet He submitted to its conditions anyway. Though

> existing in the form of God,
> [He] did not consider equality with God
> as something to be exploited. (Phil. 2:6)

He did not take advantage of His rights as God or hold them up as an exemption card so He wouldn't have to stoop to become like us.

Instead,

> he emptied himself
> by assuming the form of a servant,
> taking on the likeness of humanity. (v. 7)

Twentieth-century theologian A. W. Pink put it this way: "He drew a veil over His glory that He might remove our reproach."[13] It was an action so incomparably humble that it removes any excuse we could ever make for having a prideful attitude, acting entitled, or demanding our own rights.

Jesus walked in our skin. He showed us what mankind, created in the image of God, was meant to be—wholly human, fully obedient to God, living in the joy and fullness of relationship with Him.

How does the humanity of Jesus make a difference in your perspective on your own humanity?

What do you see in Jesus that helps you better understand what God created us as humans to be?

Lord Jesus, there are so many reasons to love You. How can I not love You most for this? For humbling Yourself. For willingly taking on human flesh and considering us worth the cost. When I feel disrespected or taken advantage of, help me choose the pathway of humility as You did. You laid aside Your glory for me. May I live to give You the glory You deserve.

AMEN.

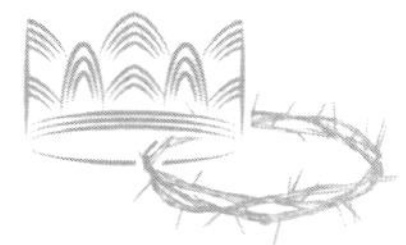

Day 12

Courage under Control

The Manliness of Christ

"Behold the Man!"
—JOHN 19:5 NKJV

As a test of how deeply our world and its hypersensitivities have gotten inside our heads, notice whether you sense a whiff of controversy when I make the following (obviously accurate) statement: Jesus was not just a human; Jesus was a man. A male.

Yesterday we looked at Jesus' humanity—something He shared in common with both men and women. As He obeyed the Father and resisted temptation, He modeled qualities that should be true of all believers, both male and female.

But He exhibited that obedience as a man, not as a woman or some androgynous being. And His manhood was not an arbitrary aspect of His incarnation. God didn't flip a coin to decide whether Jesus should be born as male or female. The maleness of Jesus was necessary and significant in God's redemptive plan. Most Old Testament prophets were men. All priests and kings were men. And Christ fulfills the Old Testament types of prophet, priest, and king. For these (and other) reasons, He had to be a man.

Jesus also lived out His humanity in distinctively masculine ways. He was not only the perfect human being, but also the perfect male. As such, He provides the perfect role model for all men.

In the Gospels we see His gracious masculinity in His treatment of women. Unlike many in His culture, He was respectful toward them. He considered them worthy of having their personhood acknowledged, their dignity protected, their voices heard. He wasn't standoffish or awkward around them, nor was He manipulative or controlling in His dealings with them. To anyone who's ever been hurt or abandoned or betrayed by a male figure, anyone who has lamented broken, toxic masculinity in our culture, prepare to find in Jesus perfect faithfulness, perfect understanding, perfect honor, perfect love. Perfect manhood.

But what exactly does that mean? After all, people's concept of ideal manhood has fluctuated throughout history and across cultures. Should a man be tireless, active, decisive, powerful? Tender, gentle, compassionate, quiet? A good protector? A good listener?

Yes. And Jesus was all those things in perfect balance.

He could be direct, even pointed, in conversation, but He was also patient and approachable. Judging by the way He overturned the merchants' tables in the temple (John 2:13–17), He could be confrontational; He certainly was not afraid to get His message across. But He was also gentle and measured. "He will not argue or shout," He said of Himself, quoting the prophet Isaiah,

> and no one will hear his voice in the streets.
> He will not break a bruised reed,
> and he will not put out a smoldering wick. (Matt. 12:19–20)

Jesus knew when to whisper, just as He knew when to raise His voice. He knew when to extend mercy and when to exact judgment. People knew He meant business, but they also knew without a doubt that He meant love. He was "full of grace and truth" (John 1:14). He was (and is) everything in one package—a true Man.

He flawlessly lived out the challenge, given by Paul later in the New Testament, to "act like men, be strong" (1 Cor. 16:13 ESV)—or, as rendered in the CSB: "Be courageous, be strong." It brings to mind God's exhortation to Joshua in the Old Testament: "Be strong and courageous" (Josh. 1:9).

Truly, is there any better model of strength and courage than Jesus?

How strong and brave did He need to be to stand up to the Pharisees, the undisputed religious leaders in the Jewish community? And what great strength and courage it took for Him to tell His disciples that He must "go to Jerusalem and suffer many things from the elders, chief priests, and scribes, be killed, and be raised the third day" (Matt. 16:21).

Some of them, Peter most loudly, protested, "Oh no, Lord! This will never happen to you!" (v. 22). But Jesus was stronger than those who naïvely defended Him, stronger than those who maliciously convicted Him. In fulfillment of ancient prophecy, He "set [His] face like flint" (Isa. 50:7) and headed straight into the stiff headwinds that opposed His purpose. He stayed firm, fixed, and steadfast. Strong and courageous all the way.

Compare Him to Adam. Adam was set up to be the perfect man. He was placed in an ideal setting and given ready-made opportunities for stepping up into his God-given calling. Yet in the first real challenge of his life—the first one we're told about in Scripture, at least—Adam was AWOL. Though he was physically present with his wife, Eve, when she was targeted by the serpent's deceptions (Gen. 3:6), he apparently stood by as a passive observer, conspicuously silent when his wisdom, initiative, and loving leadership mattered most. He failed to protect her and intervene. Instead of leading, he lagged weakly behind.

How different Jesus is from that picture. Not only in His earthly life, but still today, Christ gives us a pattern for true manliness as the Savior, Head, and Bridegroom of His church. As the second Adam, He stepped in to reverse the effects of the first Adam's failure to protect and provide spiritual leadership for the woman.

Jesus' manliness is seen in His pursuit of His bride, the church—wooing and winning her heart and, in His uncommon, selfless, sacrificial love, laying down His life for her. Even now He leads and loves and shepherds her and faithfully provides for her. He rescues her from danger and delivers her from evil. He is always working for her well-being and has planned all that is needed for her eternal joy.

These are the kinds of things real men do for those under their care. And Jesus is the supreme model for what that looks like.

Does this mean only men should be inspired by His example? Is it wrong for women to value having strength and courage? Of course not. It simply means we have for our inspiration the perfect Man. Jesus got it right when it came to living out His manhood. And by His Spirit within us He can enable us to live out our manhood and womanhood to the glory of God.

That said, let us be mindful that Christ is the only perfect man who has ever lived. We cannot expect other men to be what only He can be. So, with the woman at the well (who knew an imperfect man when she saw one), let us urge others to "come see a man" (John 4:29) who is like none other.

When people see Him in His deity, in His flawless humanity, and yes, in His manliness, how can they not be drawn to Him?

How does the manliness of Christ bless His bride, the church?

How does the perfect manhood of Jesus encourage or inspire you as a man/woman?

Our Father, in a day when there is such confusion about and resistance to Your good plan for men and women, thank You for the gift of Your Son, who models what it means to mirror Your image as a man and to honor and care for women, equally created in Your image.

AMEN.

Day 13

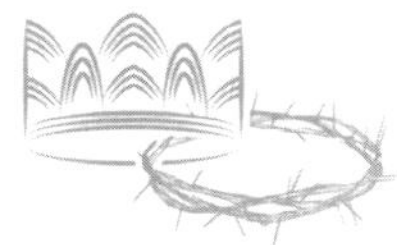

Pondering the Paradox

The Twofold Nature of Christ

When the time came to completion,
God sent his Son, born of a woman.
—GALATIANS 4:4

Why does sin retain such a hold and appeal for you and me? We could lose our minds trying to figure that one out.

The sins that tempt us most have proven to be our worst enemies, causing us more trouble and mischief than anything else in our lives. And yet—at all the wrong times and in all the wrong ways—we somehow find them attractive. Sensible. Comfortable. Preferable.

How can that be?

After many years and many hard failings, here's what I've concluded to be my best answer: sin becomes attractive to the extent that I take my eyes off Jesus.

And the opposite is true as well. The more I see of Him, the more I get to know Him and learn to love Him, the less alluring sin's temptations become. My battles feel less overwhelming as I grow more captivated by the greatness and beauty of who He is.

So when you and I ponder the foundational truths of the nature and work of Christ, as we are doing in these reflections, we're not doing it to breathe the rarefied air of scholarly musings. Nor should we be daunted when some of those concepts seem complex and difficult or conclude that they are not really useful or practical to our daily lives.

Truth is, these cosmic realities matter greatly in daily life. As we seek to grasp them, even in their mystery, they draw forth worship and awe from us, from breathless hearts grown weary under the loads we carry. They make us want more of this One who loves us, and want fewer of those things—in fact, *none* of those things—that propose to help us but only hurt us.

Take, for example, the perplexity that can arise when we pair Christ's *divinity* with His *humanity*. Throughout the first few centuries AD, debate raged over how to synthesize these seemingly paradoxical claims. How could Jesus be both divine and human? At the same time? In the same person?

The resulting arguments created feuding camps among religious leaders and teachers, some of whom defended ideas like these (later held to be heresies):

1. Christ was a highly exalted being but not fully God.
2. He had a human body but not a human mind and spirit.
3. He was two different persons (one human, one divine) in one body.
4. He was an equal mixture of the two (partially human, partially divine).

After generations of such squabbles, hashed out in gathered assemblies of church representatives from all over the known world, a fourth council convened in AD 451 in the city of Chalcedon. And out of this extended meeting of the minds, as they dived back into the Scriptures to see what God's Spirit had revealed about the Son, they developed what became known as the Chalcedonian Creed, which can be summarized by the following four statements:

1. Christ is fully and completely divine (fully God).
2. He is fully and completely human (fully man).
3. His divine and human natures are distinct (not mixed together).
4. His divine and human natures are completely united in one person.

This is one of the most profound concepts in theology, beyond our ability to grasp fully. But should we really expect Jesus to be any less? This is what makes Him *incomparable*.

Jesus is fully divine, *and* He is fully human. He existed as God before time began, but He took on a human nature when conceived by the Holy Spirit in Mary's womb, without in any way diminishing His deity.

This is affirmed in Isaiah's Messianic prophecy:

> For unto us a Child is born [*humanity*],
> Unto us a Son is given [*deity*]. (Isa. 9:6 NKJV)

In the New Testament we read that "God sent his Son, born of a woman" (Gal. 4:4). One and the same Person, yet with two natures. Fully God, fully man.

We see both natures evident in the Gospels: Jesus could attend a wedding (a human activity), but while there He could change water into wine (a divine activity). He could be weary enough to fall asleep in a boat with His disciples (a human characteristic), but when awakened He could rebuke a storm and calm the seas (a divine characteristic).

And this twofold nature is not temporary, but permanent. Jesus is *still* the God-man and will be forever. Today He is enthroned in heaven in His resurrected, glorified body, with (as many Bible students believe) the scars of the nails and spear still visible in His hands and side.[14]

Is your head spinning a little? You're not alone. This mystery has challenged Christians in every era. But consider this:

If Jesus is anything less than fully human and fully divine, He is not enough for us. This twofold nature of Christ is absolutely essential if our redemption is to be accomplished.

if Jesus is anything less than fully human and fully divine, He is not enough for us. This twofold nature of Christ is absolutely essential if our redemption is to be accomplished. "The union of Christ's deity and humanity in one Person," writes author Matt Perman, "makes it such that we have all that we need in the same Savior."[15]

The humanity of Christ means He is *willing* to save us.

The divinity of Christ means He is *able* to save us.

Both willing and able—that's what we need. And that's what we have in Jesus.

And remember that the entrance of this God-man into the world was for *us*. "Unto *us* a Child is born" and "unto *us* a Son is given." We were sinners, enemies of God, separated from Him. And Jesus—without ceasing to be fully God, without laying aside any of his Godness—took on our human nature that He might reconcile us to the Father. What a wonder this is! What love this is!

Why should we ever feel the need to look for completion, for comfort, for temporary solutions in ourselves, in our sins, or anywhere else, when we have such a Savior?

Why does it matter that Jesus is one Person with two natures: fully God and fully human?

How could the difference between staring down temptation and staring into the eyes of your Savior be significant in your life?

Father, I praise You for the mystery and the wonder of who Jesus is: fully God, yet fully human. He is everything I need and more in time and eternity. Not only was He willing to save me; He is also able to save me from the power and practice of my sin. Who else could ever be as lovely and desirable as He is to me?

AMEN.

Day 14

Unblemished

The Sinlessness of Christ

He was revealed so that he might take away sins,
and there is no sin in him.
—1 JOHN 3:5

Jesus never sinned.

If you've grown up in the church, as I have, you might think this goes without saying. But surveys show that many contemporary Americans aren't so sure. In fact, close to half of the population disagrees with that statement. Among adult churchgoers the percentage is not always much better.[16]

So maybe it makes sense to take a closer look at this assertion about Jesus, asking two important questions:

- Is it true?
- Why does it matter?

It's hard to be any clearer about Jesus' sinless nature than John the apostle was. After all, he had spent three full years with Jesus, observing Him night and day in situations that ran the gamut from highly stressful to completely unguarded. Yet John reported there was "no sin in him" (1 John 3:5). So did Simon Peter, who declared, "He did not commit sin" (1 Peter 2:22).

Jesus Himself claimed to be without sin. To those who *thought* He was sinning—that is, failing to conform to their faulty interpretation of God's law—He answered, "The one who sent me [God Himself] is with me, because I always do what pleases him" (John 8:29). Shortly before His death He repeated the claim: "I have kept my Father's commands" (John 15:10). He even laid down a challenge to His opponents, asking, "Who among you can convict me of sin?" (John 8:46).

No one dared take Him up on it. In fact, some of Jesus' enemies and even some unbiased observers attested to His sinless life.

- Pilate: "I find no grounds for charging this man" (Luke 23:4).
- Judas: "I have sinned by betraying innocent blood" (Matt. 27:4).
- The thief on the cross: "This man has done nothing wrong" (Luke 23:41).
- Demonic spirits: "I know who you are—the Holy One of God!" (Luke 4:34).

From a biblical standpoint, then, the case for Jesus' sinlessness is indisputable. But what about the second question: Why does it matter?

It matters because *we are not sinless.*

The instant that Adam and Eve, the first humans, chose to disobey God, sin became encoded into the human DNA. "Through one man's disobedience the many were made sinners" (Rom. 5:19), doomed to pass down Adam's original sin to every child born of human parents. So each of us came into this world with a sinful nature:

- "I was sinful when my mother conceived me" (Ps. 51:5).
- "There is no one righteous, not even one" (Rom. 3:10).
- "All have sinned and fall short of the glory of God" (Rom. 3:23).

Which means we all need a Savior—a *sinless* Savior.

We need Jesus, who did what Adam failed to do. Who perfectly obeyed the law of God. Who was "tempted . . . yet without sin" (Heb. 4:15).

It's hard for us to fathom how a man, even Jesus as a man, could remain sinless for an entire lifetime. You and I can't go a day; He did it for more than three decades. How was it possible that He did not have a sinful nature like that of every other human who has ever lived?

Human life begins at the point of conception—the moment the DNA of a man and woman are joined together. But the baby Jesus born in Bethlehem was not the product of the physical union of a man and a woman. He was supernaturally conceived in Mary's womb by the power of the Holy Spirit (Luke 1:35), so that no sin was transmitted to Him from Mary or Joseph.

This is why the virgin birth is so vital. It's what makes it possible for Christ to share our humanity (born of a woman) without sharing our sinful nature (conceived by the Holy Spirit). And that matters immensely because it is integral to Jesus' mission of reclaiming us from the curse of sin—the very reason He came to earth!

The virgin birth makes it possible for Christ to share our humanity (born of a woman) without sharing our sinful nature (conceived by the Holy Spirit). It is integral to Jesus' mission of reclaiming us from the curse of sin.

You see, as the sinless Son of God, Jesus was able to offer Himself up as a sacrifice for our sin, stunningly fulfilling a powerful picture that would have been well-known to every Israelite in His day.

Since the early days of God's covenant with His chosen people, worshipers had been required to offer animals as sacrifices to make atonement for their sins. Day after day, year after year, lambs "without blemish" or defect (Ex. 12:5) were killed and their blood poured out before God. Day after day, year after year, innocent lambs by the thousands died the death that sinners deserved.

After centuries of these lambs being slain and sacrificed in the place of sinners, imagine that moment when John looked up from baptizing people at the Jordan River, saw Jesus approaching, and with wonder and awe pointed Him out to the crowd: "Look, the Lamb of God, who takes away the sin of the world!" (John 1:29). What must have gone through the minds of those at the scene?

They knew that in order to take away sin, a lamb had to be perfect, and it had to die. Now, before their eyes, stood the sinless Lamb of God who would die for the sins of the world. The perfect Substitute.

The Son of God had no sin to mar His record; He was completely innocent, unblemished. Falsely accused, He died a death He did not deserve, the death we rightly deserved for our sin. He is the perfect sacrifice who alone could atone for that sin. And, wonder of wonders, we have been declared righteous because of His death in our place. "For Christ also suffered for sins once for all, the righteous for the unrighteous, that he might bring you to God" (1 Peter 3:18).

This was the mission He came to fulfill, and He completed it perfectly. God "made the one who did not know sin to be sin for us, so that in him we might become the righteousness of God" (2 Cor. 5:21).

Yes, until His transforming, sanctifying work in us is complete, the sin that indwells our natural flesh will keep rearing its ugly head, but—here's the good news—we no longer have to live under sin's control.

We have a way out, thanks to our sinless Christ.

Why did Jesus have to be sinless in order to be our Savior?

What difference does the sinlessness of Christ make in our battle against sin?

Dear Lamb of God, How grateful I am that You, the sinless One, died for sinful people like me, that we might be declared righteous in the sight of God. You are worthy of all my worship and love.

AMEN.

Day 15

Weight of Glory

The Transfiguration of Christ

"I want those you have given me to be with me where I am, so that they will see my glory."

—JOHN 17:24

Jesus spent every day of His life in the shadow of the cross. It was always out there in front of Him: the rejection, the humiliation, the unthinkable suffering, the gruesome death.

His followers, on the other hand, saw His miracles, His wisdom, His winsome way with people, and His clear connection with His heavenly Father. And the closer they came to recognizing that He was truly their Messiah, the more mystified they grew at His repeated predictions of doom and gloom—of being hauled away, beaten, tortured, killed. How could this possibly be true? The Messiah's job was to lead them to victory, to conquer their oppressors, to guide His people to a new day of freedom, to make everything all better. His coming was supposed to be glorious, not grievous.

Well, they were half right.

One night during a mountaintop retreat, three of His disciples were awakened from sleep by the blaze of a brilliant light. Jesus, who had been praying while these three companions slept (not an uncommon occurrence, we come to find out) had begun radiating like a lightning flash. It wasn't as though a spotlight had been focused on Him; rather, blazing light emanated from within Him. "His face shone like the sun" (Matt. 17:2), "and his clothes became dazzling—extremely white as no launderer on earth could whiten them" (Mark 9:3).

Glory!—more glory than they could ever imagine, a scene of such eye-popping amazement they would never forget it. "We were eyewitnesses of his majesty," one of them would later write in recalling this event (2 Peter 1:16). "We observed his glory, the glory as the one and only Son from the Father," another would recall (John 1:14).

Then, as if seeing Jesus Himself in such a glorified state were not enough, the disciples realized that two other men were standing alongside Him, "talking with him" (Matt. 17:3). Somehow they identified the newcomers as two towering spiritual giants who had played unique roles in the history of Israel: Moses the great lawgiver, whose face reflected the glory of God when he came down from being in the presence of God, and Elijah the prophet, who did not die but was transported alive to heaven in a chariot of fire, prefiguring the ascension of Jesus into heaven.

In this moment the disciples were given a glimpse of the glory Jesus had enjoyed in heaven before He came to earth, the glory He'd temporarily laid aside to take on human flesh.

The disciples were undone. Peter, "not knowing what he was saying" (Luke 9:33), babbled on about building a mountain lodge or something, a place that could accommodate the whole group of them, where they could all just stay up on the mountain forever. He never wanted to come down.

Yet cutting through this chatter—like a royal "Be quiet!"—came the clincher. "Suddenly a bright cloud covered them, and a voice from the cloud said, 'This is my beloved Son, with whom I am well-pleased. Listen to him!'" (Matt. 17:5).

Stand in awe with me—and with Peter, James, and John—at this glorious event. This was the one occasion during Jesus' earthly life when the fullness of the Godhead shone through the veil of His humanity. In this moment the disciples were given a glimpse of the glory Jesus had enjoyed in heaven before He came to earth, the glory He'd temporarily laid aside to take on human flesh. They were given a preview of the glorified body that would be His following His death and resurrection and of the unclouded glory that will radiate from Him for all eternity.

And from this mountain—henceforth to be known as the Mount of Transfiguration—Jesus could easily have called an end to the cross-heavy burden He'd been sent here to endure. What was keeping Him from returning right then to be with the Father whose voice they all heard, to sit and reign with Him forever?

But the conversation the three disciples overheard between Moses, Elijah, and Jesus wasn't about the glories of heaven that lay ahead for Jesus. Rather, they were "speaking of his departure"—His *death*—"which he was about to accomplish in Jerusalem" (Luke 9:31). Apparently they knew what Jesus also knew:

- Before His exaltation must come His humiliation.
- Only after His humiliation could come His vindication.

There would be no glory without a cross.

Jesus and these two Old Testament heroes had a laser focus on His "departure." The Greek word used here is *exodos,* which we immediately recognize as being related to our English word *exodus.* And that's a subject Moses knew a thing or two about. When the children of Israel found themselves in slavery to cruel Egyptian taskmasters, God had raised Moses up as a deliverer to lead His oppressed people out of bondage. But the Old Testament exodus was intended to point toward a New Testament exodus, a mission to be led by an even greater Deliverer. Its purpose? To redeem us from our bondage to an even more sinister tyrant—human sin.

So, even here on this Mount of Transfiguration, amid these stunning sights and sounds of heavenly transport, the cross remained the central feature. Just as on all the other nights and early mornings in Jesus' life, His future suffering on the cross was uppermost in His mind.

Once again we see His submission and sacrifice in His choice not to return to heaven from the mountaintop ecstasy, but to walk back down that mountain to the valley below, where He would face dire human need, demonic forces, sickness, sin, and death. And where He Himself would soon be put to death.

"Let's stay right here," exclaimed Peter, basking in the euphoria of the moment. (And who could blame him?) But God's plan for His Son was the cross. And rather than clinging to the indescribable wonder of that hallowed mount, Jesus gladly said yes to the will of His Father, knowing that the glory yet to come must be preceded by His death for sin.

The same cross that had brought Him down from heaven brought Him obediently down from this mountaintop.

So that we, because of His cross, could taste His glory.

What are some glimpses of glory that God has graciously given to encourage you on your journey here on earth?

What is one way you are being called to follow the example of Jesus by enduring hardship here on earth, waiting for a promised reward yet to come?

God of glory, I worship You. Thank You for this glimpse of Jesus clothed in glory. And thank You that He was willing to lay aside His rights and humble Himself to the point of death on the cross. May I, by "looking as in a mirror at the glory of the Lord," be "transformed into the same image from glory to glory" (2 Cor. 3:18). Blessing, honor, glory, and praise be to You.

AMEN.

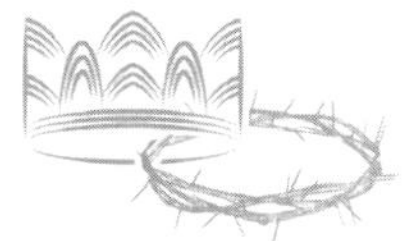

Day 16

Thus Says the Lord

The Prophetic Ministry of Christ

"The LORD your God will raise up for you a prophet."
—DEUTERONOMY 18:15

They knew they were waiting for a prophet.

The Prophet.

Moses, one of the greatest Old Testament prophets, had been the first to declare it.

In Deuteronomy 18, Moses had urged the people not to be like the pagan nations around them, who looked to fortune-tellers and sorcerers for direction. Instead, they were to listen to God. But the voice of God was understandably terrifying to a sinful people. In fact, at the original giving of the law on Mount Sinai, the people of Israel had begged, "Let us not continue to hear the voice of the LORD our God or see this great fire any longer, so that we will not die!" (Deut. 18:16).

Fearful of being consumed by the presence and glory of God, the people wanted Him to speak to them through a human intermediary like Moses. A prophet.

The Lord, hearing their request, declared His intention to honor it. But then He promised Moses that He would "raise up for them a Prophet" (v. 18 NKJV) who would be like Moses in many respects—a teacher, ruler, deliverer—only greater. It was through this ultimate Prophet that God would make Himself and His will known to His people:

> "I . . . will put My words in his mouth, and He shall speak to them all that I command Him." (v. 18 NKJV)

Yes, a prophet had come. Moses.

But *the* Prophet was still yet to come.

As one generation followed another beyond the exodus, new prophets emerged onto the stage of Jewish history, each defined by the same qualities:

- *They were chosen and sent by God.* They didn't appoint themselves to the office.
- *God spoke to them,* revealing His will, telling them what He wanted His people to know in the form of announcements, instructions, words of comfort, and warnings.
- *The prophets listened to God.* They received His revelation.
- *They proclaimed the message they had received.* They were not to speak their own words or thoughts, but whatever He directed them to say to His people. "Thus says the Lord" was their message.

And yet even as prophets like Elijah, Isaiah, and Jeremiah fulfilled their prophetic role, the belief persisted—based on the promise in Deuteronomy—that Someone greater was coming. In fact, many of the prophets themselves pointed toward His coming. This Prophet would be the Messiah, the One to lead God's people, to teach them and counsel them and deliver them in ways even greater than Moses had done. Each successive generation eagerly anticipated His arrival.

Then, after Malachi, the prophetic word went dark. Four centuries went by without a single word from heaven. People desperately needed to know God's will and God's way. The longing for the coming of the promised One grew stronger, the expectation sharper.

That's why when you reach the days of John the Baptist, you hear the Jewish priests asking John specifically, "Are you the Prophet?" (John 1:21). John's answer was no, but people knew to keep looking. And some of those who heard the teaching of Jesus and observed His miracles and wonders were keen to voice their conclusions: "This truly is the Prophet" (John 7:40)—the One "who is to come into the world" (John 6:14).

The more people heard from Him, the more readily they could tell He was performing the twin practices of the prophetic role:

- *foretelling*: declaring events that were still to come, such as His sufferings and death, His resurrection, the destruction of Jerusalem, His second coming, and the final judgment
- *forth-telling*: making known the character, heart, and wisdom of God; explaining the law and the gospel; preaching good news to the poor

Not just as *a* prophet, as some religions have called Him, but as *the* Prophet.

Jesus Himself claimed that the message He brought had been received from God:

> "For I have not spoken on my own, but the Father himself who sent me has given me a command to say everything I have said." (John 12:49)

Jesus was and is God's final Spokesman. His Word is authoritative and true. When Moses foretold the coming of this Prophet, he said: "You must listen to him" (Deut. 18:15). And God further warned: "I will hold accountable whoever does not listen to my words that he speaks in my name" (v. 19).

"All the prophets who have spoken," Peter would later say, "from Samuel and those after him, have . . . foretold these days" (Acts 3:24)—these very days of Jesus and His unique role as Messiah. The writer of Hebrews put it this way: "Long ago God spoke to our ancestors by the prophets at different times and in different ways. In these last days, he has spoken to us by his Son" (Heb. 1:1–2).

And though more than two millennia have passed since then, you and I remain in that audience. We have the Father's affirmation of Jesus as His Son on the Mount of Transfiguration. We have the example of His life and the recorded fulfillment of every word He spoke about Himself on the earth. And "we also have the prophetic word strongly confirmed," as Peter declared, and we "will do well to pay attention to it, as to a lamp shining in a dark place, until the day dawns and the morning star rises in your hearts" (2 Peter 1:19).

No other word is coming. No other word is necessary. Christ, the promised Prophet, anointed and sent by God, has shown us the will and mind and purposes of God. We have it in the Scriptures, and it has been revealed to us by the Holy Spirit. Our job now is to listen to Him, to believe and obey His Word, and to proclaim it to others, for He said to His followers: "As the Father has sent me, I also send you" (John 20:21).

Even people who knew Jesus well during His earthly life often failed to take His prophetic message to heart. How can you cultivate and maintain a heart that believes and pays close attention to His Word?

We live in a pluralistic world that rejects absolute truth and encourages people to find their own "truth." Why can you be confident and unafraid when you share the Word of Christ with others?

Thank You, Father, for going to such lengths to communicate Your truth to Your people, through the words of the prophets of old and in these "last days" through your Son, Jesus. Help me to listen to Him, to pay careful attention to His Word, to believe it, and to worship Him as the supreme Prophet, not just one among many.

AMEN.

Day 17

Astonishing Words

The Teaching of Christ

They were astonished at his teaching because he was teaching them as one who had authority.

—MARK 1:22

I was one of those odd kids who absolutely loved school. I always enjoyed sitting and listening to my teachers—well, almost always—and wanted to be a teacher when I grew up.

Since those early days I've had the opportunity to study under many teachers—some whose superb communication skills kept me on the edge of my seat, some whose knowledge and intellect went over my head, and a few who, to be honest, were just plain hard to listen to for very long.

I've also had the joy of teaching God's Word for many years now, so I understand the effort it takes to organize what often feel like stray thoughts into something meaningful, something that clearly communicates His truth. I know the challenge of connecting to the hearts of listeners in a way that is life-giving and life-changing.

With all that in mind, I'd like to consider with you what it must have been like to hear Jesus teach.

He was a master teacher, after all. In fact, Teacher is one of the main titles His followers gave Him. He must have been amazing to hear.

That's the one word—*amazed* (along with its equivalent, *astonished*)—that the Gospel writers most often employed to describe how people felt when they heard Him minister in person. Some, of course, were "offended" by Him (Matt. 13:57), either by how unconventional

He was or by His freedom to speak unpopular truth that targeted the hypocrisy in people's hearts. But even the ones He offended couldn't help being astounded by the things He said and the way He said them.

For those who are deeply familiar with Jesus' story, it may be hard to comprehend just how refreshingly different He sounded to His listeners, how much His teaching style contrasted with what they were accustomed to hearing. The scribes and rabbis and other religious teachers of the day spent their lives studying and dissecting the minute details of the Mosaic law. Straining out gnats is what Jesus called it (Matt. 23:24). He, however, taught about issues that really mattered—the kingdom of God, the King who reigns over it, and the enormity of purpose, freedom, and abundance that people could experience from Him.

Jesus' teaching is timeless; it never becomes obsolete. It is eternally relevant—to every person in every culture in every time period of history.

Jesus didn't rely on borrowed sources either. That's another thing that amazed His listeners. They were accustomed to teachers who leaned heavily on tradition and precedent, on quoted references from what others had said in the past. But Jesus taught "like one who had authority, and not like their scribes" (Matt. 7:29). He knew what He was talking about.

Though He wasn't formally trained, though He'd spent His formative years as a tradesman, He knew the Scriptures—not just the words but the wisdom. (By my count, He referenced passages from as many as twenty-four Old Testament books in His teaching and conversations as recorded in the Gospels.) And He knew how they applied to the lives of His listeners. When the truth He taught landed on people who genuinely wanted to hear, His words carried instant credibility.

They radiated another quality too: genuine love. Think how often the sermons of the scribes were delivered only to impress, to rack up scholarly credits, to inflate their own sense of superiority with the hot air of their lecturing. But Jesus' concern was for His listeners—to engage their attention, to capture their imaginations, to touch their hearts with the truth. Instead of overwhelming them with His intellect, He taught them with stories and word pictures that they could relate to, keeping it all so direct and simple that even a child could follow.

Why? Because He truly cared about the people in His audience. He knew their hearts. He knew what they needed. And He wanted them to know the Father's love as He did.

So where other teachers rambled, Jesus got straight to the point.

Where other teachers were hard to follow, He was orderly and sensible.

Where they waxed complex, He spoke with purity and clarity.

Where they hid behind words, He lived what He taught.

His teaching is timeless; it never becomes obsolete. It is eternally relevant—to every person in every culture in every time period of history.

And though Jesus *drew* large numbers of listeners, He didn't *pursue* large numbers. Even in His epic Sermon on the Mount, the impression given to us in Scripture is that He started by talking with a small gathering of His disciples (Matt. 5:1), which grew over time into crowds (Matt. 7:28) as interested listeners drew closer to hear.

In fact, Jesus spent most of His time not preaching to crowds but interacting with His little group of twelve, often just a core group of three. In such intimate settings Jesus wove eternal truth into everyday moments. He let His followers ask questions. He steered ordinary conversations into opportunities for talking about God's perspective on themes both timely and timeless.

And there, I believe, is where we do our most effective teaching too—for we all are called to be teachers, whether or not we do it professionally. The author of Hebrews said it this way: "Although by this time you ought to be teachers, you need someone to teach you the basic principles of God's revelation again" (Heb. 5:12). We are to be not just *recipients,* but also *conduits* of Christ's teaching—always passing on to others what we've learned from Him.

Our homes, our dinner tables, our small groups, even our most casual interactions are teaching places. People may not fill up their notebooks with the things we say, but God can speak in up-close ways through people like us who love Him and His Word and who truly care for the spiritual well-being of those around us.

As Jesus did. When Jesus taught.

What kind of authority and weight does Jesus' teaching carry in your life? Do you sit in awe of His Word, aware that when Christ speaks, God speaks?

What are some of the places in your life that you'd never really thought of as being teaching opportunities, where you might share with others what you have learned from Him?

Thank You, Father, for sending Jesus to be our Teacher. In Him we see not only the methods of effective teaching but its heart—Your heart. May I never stop being a student of Jesus and Your Word. And may I be alert to opportunities to use what You've taught me to help teach others Your truth.

AMEN.

Day 18

The Root of Every Virtue

The Humility of Christ

"Learn from me, because I am . . . humble in heart,
and you will find rest for your souls."
—MATTHEW 11:29

Theologians, in describing God's being and character, often differentiate between what they call His *incommunicable* attributes and His *communicable* ones. Those big words simply mean that some of God's qualities belong to God alone and some He lets us share with Him, though obviously to a lesser degree.

Incommunicable traits are ones we can never have, like omniscience or omnipresence or Christ's sinless perfection.

Communicable traits are those we can and should aspire to, like love, mercy, compassion.

And *humility*, which is one of the characteristics that make Jesus truly *incomparable*. It's also one He invites us to experience with Him, to participate in, and to grow in, becoming more like Him in the process.

The Christian ideal of humility was a revolutionary concept in the ancient world. The Greeks didn't even have a word for it. The closest they came in their culture was the idea of being *lowly*, but such lowliness carried a meaning more like being timid, weak, and cowardly—which didn't describe Jesus at all.

So in His teaching on humility—and, more importantly, in His embodiment of humility—Jesus was championing something that many of those around Him had never thought to appreciate or desire.

He transformed a human quality they considered a weakness or even a vice into a virtue—what Andrew Murray once called "the root of every virtue."[17] Because true humility as modeled by Jesus is the opposite of pride, which we know from Scripture is at the root of every sin.

Adam and Eve's pride, their self-exaltation, their sense of human entitlement, their desire not to be confined by God's directives, is what severed their relationship with God in the garden, and we humans have been suffering from this toxic quality ever since. Trace back every failing you've ever experienced, whether in your own life or that of others, and tell me if its source is not found in an elevation of self, an unholy desire for what we want, an unwillingness to wait on God or submit to His Word.

Yet trace through the life of Jesus, and you see humility everywhere. He of all people had reason to be proud, and yet He repeatedly demonstrated just the opposite. For example:

1. Jesus left the majesty and splendor of heaven and came to this earth to take on human flesh.

Without pomp or fanfare, He was born to a poor teenage girl under humble circumstances. He laid aside His rights and privileges as God and the independent exercise of His divine attributes—surely the most profound act of humility ever pondered or put into action.

2. Jesus did not seek honor or praise from others.

He, of course, was worthy of all glory, and He received glory and affirmation from His Father. But He didn't look for it or angle for it from anyone else (John 8:50). He knew that human praise and honor could not sustain Him, any more than it can sustain us. So He didn't even try to "accept glory from people" (John 5:41).

3. Jesus lived in total dependence on His heavenly Father.

Nothing that existed in the physical world was beyond His power to control and make personal use of. And yet He obligated Himself to do only what His Father told Him or showed Him to do, humbly placing His Father's plans above His own. "The Son is not able to do anything on his own," he insisted, "but only what he sees the Father doing" (John 5:19). As a result, He said, "I do nothing on my own authority" (John 8:28 ESV) and "I seek not my own will but the will of him who sent me" (John 5:30 ESV).

4. Rather than being self-seeking, Jesus placed the needs of others above His own.

His disciples, heady with being part of the Messiah's inner circle, could often be heard squabbling with one another, competing over which of them was the greatest. But Jesus gently reminded them: "Whoever wants to become great among you will be your servant" (Mark 10:43)—an example He lived out consistently, quietly, humbly. "For even the Son of Man did not come to be served," He said, "but to serve, and to give his life" (v. 45).

Trace through the life of Jesus, and you see humility everywhere.

Jesus' humility was evident when He stooped like the lowest of servants to wash the disciples' feet; when He rode an ordinary donkey into Jerusalem in fulfillment of Old Testament prophecy (Zech. 9:9); when He was maligned, slandered, and falsely accused and refused to retaliate or defend Himself. And as the ultimate expression of His humility,

> He humbled himself by becoming obedient
> to the point of death—
> even to death on a cross. (Phil 2:8)

Amazing!

Now, we've said that humility is a communicable attribute. It's something Jesus wants to share with us for our good and especially for God's glory. So how can we cultivate this stunning virtue?

"Learn from me," He invites us, "because I am . . . humble in heart." Meditate on Him. Contemplate His humility, His servanthood, His love, the lengths to which He stooped to rescue us. Meditate on the cross. For it is in learning from Christ and choosing the pathway of humility that we will "find rest" (Matt. 11:29).

Free from the pressure of seeking popularity.

Exempt from all efforts at self-promotion.

Satisfied with God's opinion of us in Christ.

Watching the root of humility grow something truly beautiful in our souls.

Why are we drawn toward the humility we see in others, yet find it so difficult to humble ourselves?

How does the example of Jesus motivate you to choose the pathway of humility?

Holy Father, I have so much to learn from Jesus' incomparable example of humility. Forgive me for the ways I exalt myself and operate out of pride, demanding my own way. I bow myself before You today, acknowledging I have nothing to be proud of. Fill my heart with the humility of Jesus so that You may receive all the glory.

AMEN.

Day 19

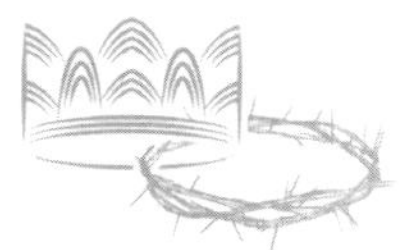

Song in the Night

The Serenity of Christ

His song will be with me in the night—
a prayer to the God of my life.
—PSALM 42:8

When's the last time you heard someone described as "serene"? *Serenity* is not a word we hear often today. It certainly doesn't describe the era in which we live. We're more familiar with hurry, crazy busyness, 24-7 multitasking, off-the-chart stress, panic attacks, and anxiety disorders. Tranquility, calmness—these are qualities people crave but find elusive. Hence the internet ad I saw once for "The Serenity Pill." *Yes! Give me one of those!* Serenity in a box, right?

Perhaps you're wishing you could slow down right now. Or be relieved from a nagging, unresolved worry. Or take your overstressed mind on a week's vacation to the beach or the mountains. Anything to get you out from under the load you're carrying or restore you to a long-lost feeling of peace and serenity. Just a little change would make all the difference.

Well, maybe.

It's true that getting away from it all can sometimes do us a world of good. For sure, sabbath observances and regular time to unplug should be part of our normal routine. The trouble is, it's not always possible to get away. And some of our worries and stresses are more than a break or vacation can handle—especially since we tend to take our troubles with us.

The truth is, a change of external circumstances can't really change the internal temperature of our hearts. If our sense of peace is governed by our current situation or surroundings, we'll have trouble summoning serenity when we need it most. So we need a better answer for how to handle our stress. And once again we can look to the incomparable Jesus to show us the way.

Many scenes throughout His earthly life come to mind:

- Jesus asleep in a boat as a storm rages on every side, then awaking and serenely calming His disciples' fears
- Jesus maintaining perfect composure in the midst of a throng of listeners assembled in a remote area with no food to eat
- Jesus keeping His composure in the throes of a grueling schedule, with people pressing in on Him from every side, making relentless demands on His time and attention
- Jesus remaining calm (though emotional) when He receives word that His dear friend Lazarus is terminally ill and subsequently dies
- Jesus responding with dignity when He is mocked, reviled, and falsely accused before a succession of religious and Roman rulers

And then in Matthew's gospel we see a particularly exquisite glimpse of the Savior's serenity—perhaps my favorite. You and I could not imagine a more taxing crisis than the one Jesus was facing the night He gathered with His disciples—including His betrayer!—in the upper room on the eve of His crucifixion. Among those celebrating this Passover meal together, He alone knew what the rest of His evening and the following day would entail. They knew *something* was different, from the way He paralleled the bread with "my body" and the cup with "my blood" (Matt. 26:26, 28). But otherwise, He followed the typical pattern for the familiar meal, even down to carrying out the traditional closing to the celebration:

After singing a hymn, they went out to the Mount of Olives. (Matt. 26:30)

Jesus was heading out into the longest, darkest night of His life. He knew He'd soon be arrested, forsaken, tortured, humiliated. He was aware that the men He'd just shared dinner with—the ones whose feet He'd washed in an act of remarkable humility—would abandon Him. If anyone ever could have felt entitled to worry, to panic, to want to escape, surely it was Jesus in this moment.

If our sense of peace is governed by our current situation or surroundings, we'll have trouble summoning serenity when we need it most.

But Jesus did none of those things. Instead, He chose to sing.

Quite likely, according to Jewish tradition, Jesus and His friends sang a song that many of them knew by heart and had known since childhood. The Hallel, or "Praise," incorporated the text from six consecutive psalms: Psalms 113–118. The first two were usually sung in the middle of the dinner, the final four at the conclusion. In totality the Hallel is a song of God's faithfulness, of His strong deliverance of His people.

So knowing the excruciating ordeal Jesus would face in the next twenty-four hours, imagine the feelings that must have washed over Him as He sang words like these:

> Not to us, Lord, not to us,
> but to your name give glory
> because of your faithful love, because of your truth. . . .
> Our God is in heaven
> and does whatever he pleases. (Ps. 115:1–3)

With these words Jesus expressed a supreme desire for the glory of God and for His will to be done on earth, regardless of what price that might mean for Him. Now, skip ahead to the last stanza of this hymn from the psalms that Jesus likely sang with His disciples:

> This is the day the LORD has made;
> let's rejoice and be glad in it. . . .
> Give thanks to the LORD, for he is good;
> his faithful love endures forever. (Ps. 118:24, 29)

Not only was Jesus *singing* as He stared down the cross. He was singing praise; He was singing a worship song. He was singing of God's goodness and His covenant-keeping love.

How could He do that? How could He sing while facing such pain and difficulty? Here's what I believe:

- He could sing because He trusted His Father.
- He could sing because He accepted and embraced His Father's plan.
- He could sing because He loved others more than He loved His own life.
- He could sing because He knew that even though the cross was just ahead, it would not be the end of the story—that the cross would lead to ultimate glory.

So what can we learn from His singing? Oswald Sanders suggested a partial answer:

> We can turn our trouble into treasure and our sorrow into song. Faith can sing her song in the darkest hour. Sorrow and singing are not incompatible.[18]

Jesus clearly understood that. And in singing praise, He found the serenity and courage to move into and through His deepest sorrow and suffering.

And so can we.

What circumstances are you facing today that threaten to steal your sense of peace and serenity?

Assuming what's going on around you won't immediately change, how could you invite God's gift of serenity into your heart right now? ***(If a particular song or hymn comes to mind, why not sing it aloud?)***

Father, what a wonder is the example of Your Son under intense pressure and stress—how He remained an oasis of calmness and confidence. Teach me to represent You in that way to others, so that they see the difference in someone whose trust is in the Lord. Help me worship and sing to You in the midst of my struggles.

AMEN.

Day 20

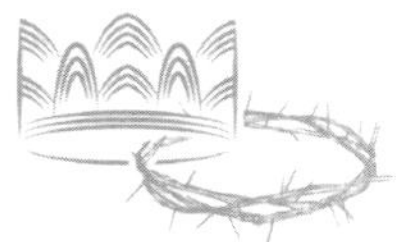

Good for Busyness

The Prayer Habits of Christ

The news about him spread even more. . . . Yet he often withdrew to deserted places and prayed.

—LUKE 5:15–16

As we journey through the Gospels, we can't help but notice that Jesus was a man of prayer. To Him, prayer meant spending time with someone He knew intimately and loved deeply and whose company He treasured. Further, in Jesus we see a man who was quick, day in and day out, to acknowledge His dependence on God.

What about us? If we truly understood how needy we are and what a privilege it is to communicate with "our Father in heaven" (Matt. 6:9), you'd think we would pray a lot. As Jesus did.

So, why don't we pray more than we do?

One reason may be that we imagine we just don't have the time—where and how are we supposed to fit prayer into our busy lives and crammed days?

It's true, of course, that life comes with a lot of responsibilities, and working hard at the tasks God has set before us is a part of stewarding our lives faithfully. But here's where the example of Jesus pushes back against the notion that the necessities of life keep us from having time for prayer. As James Stalker, a Scottish pastor from a hundred years ago, observed, "Many in our day . . . are swept off their feet with their engagements and can scarcely find time to eat. We make this a reason for not praying; Jesus made it a reason for praying."[19]

Jesus *always* found time to pray—and during His years of active ministry He was busier than any of us could ever be. Let's take just a couple of chapters from Mark's gospel as a typical window on the nonstop responsibilities and concerns that filled His days.

At the beginning of chapter 5, we see Him sailing with His disciples toward a port on the Sea of Galilee. Then we're told that "as soon as he got out of the boat, a man with an unclean spirit came out of the tombs and met him" (Mark 5:2). After delivering the man, Jesus "crossed over again by boat to the other side" (v. 21), only to be met by another large crowd, including a distraught father begging Him to come heal his young daughter, who was lying at death's door (vv. 22–24). On the way to the man's house, Jesus stopped to heal a woman who'd been "suffering from bleeding for twelve years" (v. 25).

Prayer can turn all our busy places into sacred spaces: the dinner table in our homes, the hallway with our spouse, the church aisle after Sunday services, the drive from one appointment to the next.

Leaving there, He traveled on foot "to his hometown" of Nazareth (Mark 6:1), where He taught in the synagogue before "going around the villages teaching" (v. 6). He then organized His disciples into pairs and sent them out on a mission trip, but soon He was meeting up with them again, hearing their reports, feeding five thousand people with five loaves and two fish (vv. 30–44) . . .

Jesus was one busy Man.

But even after that full day of speaking to a crowd of thousands, creating a miracle meal, and cleaning up afterward—on top of residual fatigue from long weeks without letup—He sent His disciples ahead to their next ministry location while He did what?

"He went away to the mountain to pray" (Mark 6:46).

We see this pattern again and again throughout Jesus' life. During His busiest, most pressure-packed periods, He appeared to pray *more,* not less. He operated from a mindset that caused a friend of mine to observe that "Jesus really viewed prayer as His most important work." He prayed as if He couldn't do His work without it.

- At His baptism, before the heavens opened, "he was praying" (Luke 3:21).
- Before calling His twelve disciples, He "spent all night in prayer" (Luke 6:12).
- With three disciples prior to His transfiguration, "he was praying" (Luke 9:29).

For Jesus, every occasion was an occasion for prayer—no moment too great, no moment too small, from one busy day to the next. He lived praying, and He died praying.

And if finding time for prayer still sounds impossible in your case, given all the plates you've got spinning or the limited moments you can count on being alone and quiet before Him, let's learn one other lesson from the prayer habits of Jesus: even when He couldn't "withdraw to desolate places" (Luke 5:16 ESV), when He was surrounded by the company of others, Jesus still prayed.

Once when He was "praying in a certain place" with His disciples (Luke 11:1), something they observed about His intimacy with the Father inspired them to ask, "Lord, teach us to pray" (v. 1). So He taught them what we have come to call the Lord's Prayer.

Quality prayer doesn't always require a prayer retreat. When we start to see a prayer opportunity, as Jesus did, in any place or gathering, we'll let time with the Father slice right through our busy life and make it so much more special and meaningful, so much more than just checkmarks on an agenda or an errand list. Prayer can turn all our busy places into sacred spaces: the dinner table in our homes, the hallway with our spouse, the church aisle after Sunday services, the drive from one appointment to the next.

Let's not let our busy lives keep us from regular communication with the Father. Purpose to bring Him into each task you undertake, every conversation and relational challenge, every vexing problem and unexpected interruption, every sorrowful season, and every joyous occasion.

What might be the deeper causes, beyond just the demands of your schedule, that keep you from a life of prayer?

Look for an opportunity to pray with someone the Lord brings across your path today—a family member, a coworker, a friend, or even a complete stranger.

Lord God, forgive me for being so often too busy to call out to You in prayer. Help me learn from Your Son's example that habitual prayer is not just an obligation or something to check off my list. Time spent with You is restorative and life-giving. Remind me even amid the noise and clamor of daily life that "I need Thee every hour" and that anything and everything that makes me need You is a blessing.

AMEN.

Day 21

Fervent and Faith-Filled

The Prayer Attitudes of Christ

During his earthly life, he offered prayers and appeals with loud cries and tears.

—HEBREWS 5:7

The name Hyman Appelman likely means nothing to you. It means a lot to me.

Appelman was born in 1902 into an Orthodox Jewish family in Russia. At the age of thirteen he emigrated to America, where he eventually became a trial lawyer. In 1925, as a workaholic on the brink of a breakdown, he came to faith in Christ and was disowned by his family. That was the year my father was born.

In time Appelman became an international evangelist. On October 13, 1950, my dad went to an old-time, citywide evangelistic meeting in his hometown of Albany, New York, where Appelman was preaching. That night the twenty-something young man came under conviction of his need for a Savior and was radically converted.

My dad and Dr. Appelman became dear friends. I had the privilege of hearing this venerable evangelist preach a number of times when I was a young girl. But particularly memorable to me were those few occasions when he visited our home. How I loved to sit quietly in the room, listening to conversations between my dad and this godly man with the thick Russian accent. And even more, I loved to hear him pray. There was such earnestness and passion in the way he poured out his heart to the Lord—pleading for those without Christ, interceding for the church, crying out for a moving of the Spirit here on earth.

When I recall the heartfelt prayers of both of these men, I sometimes wonder at the lack of fervency and affection in my own prayers. Why do they often seem so lackluster and lifeless by comparison? Perhaps you've felt the same.

So how can we revitalize our prayer life? There's no better way than to sit at the feet of our praying Savior. To "adopt the same attitude as that of Christ Jesus," as Paul exhorts us (Phil. 2:5).

We've already seen the humility of Christ that caused Him to live in reliance on His Father. As a man, He knew He needed God for everything, and His vibrant prayer life reflected that attitude of humble dependence. And here are three other attitudes that enlivened Jesus' prayers:

1. Jesus truly believed God heard Him when He prayed.

At times we may wonder if our petitions are actually getting through to heaven. But Jesus prayed with unblinking confidence that there really was a God who was hearing His cries.

"Father, I thank you that you heard me," He said at the tomb of Lazarus (John 11:41), knowing the enormity of what He was asking. His dear friend was dead and buried. Jesus, having removed the stone that blocked the entrance, was preparing to call Lazarus back to life from the dead—a physical impossibility. Even here He prayed with absolute certainty of being heard.

And lest we think His divinity alone is what entitled Jesus to pray with such assurance, Scripture confirms for all of us "the confidence we have before him: If we ask anything according to [God's] will, he hears us" (1 John 5:14–15). God is listening. He will answer us in His way, in His time. Truly believing this, as Jesus did, will encourage and embolden our prayer life.

2. Jesus prayed for things He knew would please and honor His Father.

He cared more about His Father's glory than about His own comfort or well-being. "My soul is troubled," He acknowledged as He thought ahead to His crucifixion, yet "what should I say—Father, save me from this hour?" (Or pray, as we often do, *Get me out of this*?) "But that is why I came to this hour," He concluded (John 12:27)—to please God, to bring Him honor. Shouldn't our prayers reflect a similar attitude at whatever cost to ourselves?

3. Even during His own Passion,[20] Jesus prayed for others.

His long prayer recorded in John 17—traditionally called His High Priestly Prayer—was delivered with the cross so near He could feel it. Yet it is marked not by apprehension about His own circumstances, but by deep love and concern for His followers.

"Protect them by your name," He asked the Father, "so that they may be one as we are one" (v. 11). "Protect them from the evil one," He also prayed (v. 15)—from being discouraged or frightened into giving up their faith. And "sanctify them by the truth" (v. 17), that they might be blessed and purified by believing what Jesus had come to do for them . . . and for us.

Yes, Jesus even prayed for you and me!

"I do not ask for these only," He said—for the eleven remaining apostles who were there in the room with Him—"but also for those who will believe in me through their word" (v. 20 ESV). That's you, and that's me. That's your kids and your grandchildren. "I want those you have given me," He prayed, "to be with me where I am, so that they will see my glory . . . so that the love you have loved me with may be in them and I may be in them" (vv. 24, 26).

God is listening. He will answer us in His way, in His time. Truly believing this, as Jesus did, will encourage and embolden our prayer life.

Jesus prayed earnest, passionate prayers. Jesus agonized in prayer. He persisted in prayer, even when He was abandoned by His Father on the cross—when the guilt He bore for our sins required our holy God to turn His gaze away. And He is praying yet today, ever present "at the right hand of God" (Rom. 8:34), living to intercede for those "who draw near to God through him" (Heb. 7:25 ESV).

Jesus is why the gates of prayer are now open to us. Jesus is why we can approach the throne with needs towering over our head and feel no shame in being desperate. Jesus is why we can come to God with nothing more tangible to offer than the tiniest seeds of faith clutched in our clasped hands and still be assured, despite whatever lack we feel, that our Father hears, our Father loves, and our Father answers.

Because Jesus, our incomparable Savior and Friend, prayed. Because Jesus believed. Because Jesus surrendered His will in humble obedience to the One whose glory He lived to magnify.

Following His example, let us pray.

Jesus told His disciples, "You can do nothing without me" (John 15:5). How could embracing this truth change your prayer life?

What do you see in Jesus' prayers that inspires you to pray with greater faith and fervency?

Thank You, Father, that You hear my prayers. And thank You for the example of Jesus, who showed us how to pray—encouraging us to be bold, permitting us to be needy, inspiring us to pray selflessly, and reminding us that Your glory is the ultimate goal of our lives and prayers.

AMEN.

Part Two

THE SAVING WORK OF CHRIST

Life is wasted if we do not grasp the glory of the cross,
cherish it for the treasure that it is,
and cleave to it as the highest price of every pleasure
and the deepest comfort in every pain.

—JOHN PIPER[21]

Day 22

Hard-Pressed

The Soul-Anguish of Christ

"I am deeply grieved to the point of death."
—MATTHEW 26:38

Everything Jesus was, everything Jesus is, everything Jesus did, led Him toward the work He was destined to do one final day. Starting one final night.

In Gethsemane.

He and His disciples had concluded their Passover meal. They'd exited the city, crossing the narrow Kidron Valley, before tucking themselves inside this garden of olive groves on the lower slopes of the Mount of Olives, just east of Jerusalem.

Gethsemane. The word comes from a Hebrew term that means "oil press"—appropriately named, because that night, among the olive trees, the Son of God would be "pressed" beyond anything we can fathom.

The traditional method of extracting oil from ripened olives is an apt metaphor for what He'd endure. The trees were thrashed so the olives would fall to the ground. Then the olives were placed in a round stone basin to be crushed and ground to a pulp through the rolling action of a large millstone. The resulting paste was smeared onto mats made of a burlap type of material. Stacking the mats one above the other, the laborers would lay a heavy collection of rocks or beams on top, further crushing the ground olives under the weight and releasing the oil in each cell, until a reddish liquid began to ooze out from the fruit.

What a picture of our Lord Jesus in that garden.

At times, when meditating again on this nighttime scene, I'm struck with a sense of how incredibly intimate it is—such a deeply personal glimpse of Jesus at a moment of intense weakness, anguish, and temptation. It almost feels like we shouldn't be allowed to witness it.

And yet Scripture invites us to look, to grapple with why He had to be put through this "olive press" of an ordeal and what it means not only to our eternal salvation but to our everyday struggles—so measly by comparison, even when they seem so mountainous.

We cannot fathom the horrors Jesus faced in Gethsemane as He contemplated the cross. We'll never know pain like what Jesus endured in that garden—a pain so unbearable that His Father mercifully assigned an angel to come be near Him—not to deliver Him from the pressure, but to bolster Him with the stamina required to pray more earnestly through His indescribable agony (Luke 22:43).

Scripture describes Jesus in those moments as "sorrowful . . . troubled . . . deeply grieved" (Matt. 26:37–38). "Deeply distressed" (Mark 14:33). And, yes, "in agony"—until "his sweat became like great drops of blood falling down to the ground" (Luke 22:44 ESV).

The Greek word translated "agony" here carries the imagery of intense competition or combat; it is sometimes used to refer to the sense of dread or apprehension a person undergoes before heading into a major fight or conflict.[22]

But why did Jesus experience such soul anguish in the face of His imminent death, when we read of others who have gone calmly to their death as martyrs, even singing on the way?

Let's be clear that those martyrs, though they may have suffered horribly for their faith, never suffered for others' sins or even for their own. They faced their crucible moments as people whose guilt and condemnation for sin had been removed by Jesus' sacrifice. But He Himself received no such relief. Our sins—your sins, my sins—were torturing Him, creating an agony unlike any other, one so intense that He cried out, "Father, if you are willing, take this cup away from me" (Luke 22:42).

He was crushed by *our* sin. Not just "sin" as a vague concept, but the cumulative dead weight of real sins—the sins of everyone who had ever lived, everyone who was yet to live. Each one of them, each sin, was heavy with its own weight of rebellion and guilt. And together they bore down on Him—piled high, pressing down. He was bowed beneath the weight of eternal judgment brought about by all that sin. And all that while He also endured the all-out assault of Satan and his demons, doing their best to get Him to refuse to carry out what the Father's redemptive plan required of Him.

Jesus was crushed by *our* sin. Not just "sin" as a vague concept, but the cumulative dead weight of real sins—the sins of everyone who had ever lived, everyone who was yet to live.

Yet despite the torture, the crushing weight of our sin, the temptation to back out of what He had come to do, Jesus stayed in that place, determined to drink every drop of that cup of judgment and wrath. To save us.

And so, when His earnest appeals to the Father brought nothing but silence from heaven, Jesus rose up from the ground, returned to His drowsy disciples—whose own sins and sleepiness only contributed to the heavy burden He bore—and said, "Get up; let's go. See, my betrayer is near" (Mark 14:42). He was prepared now, though already physically weakened by the battle, to walk right into the teeth of it.

Yes, He was pressed under the weight of our sins, yet through it all He was empowered by His reverential fear, His unswerving submission to the will of His Father, and His undying love for us sinners.

When you feel squeezed by the tempter's power, remember what you've seen here, when Christ resisted temptation on our behalf.

When your flesh wants its way, remember what you've seen here, when Christ said yes to the will of God.

When your heart aches from sin—what it's doing to you, what

it's doing to others—remember what you've seen here, when Christ drank the full cup of it so that we need not ever taste its curse.

When you wonder if you can keep pressing into the pain, remember what you've seen here.

Go to Gethsemane. Ponder the crushing He endured for your sins and mine.

And press on.

Having experienced at times a sense of the weight of guilt for your own sin, how would you begin to describe the pressure Jesus felt from carrying all our sins?

Do you sometimes tend to take sin too lightly? How do the events of Gethsemane inspire you to see your sin in a different light?

Lord Jesus, it pains me to watch You in the "olive press" of Gethsemane. My part in adding to Your agony is more than I can bear. I could never thank You enough for the depths of mercy You have shown for sinners like me. May my life bear witness to the sacrifice You have made and the price You have paid, that we might never have to be crushed by sin as You were.

AMEN.

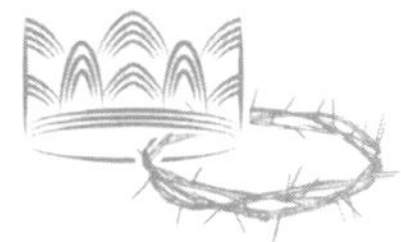

Day 23

Court of Lawbreaking

The Religious Trial of Christ

"If you are the Messiah, tell us." But he said to them,
"If I do tell you, you will not believe."
—LUKE 22:67

Jesus prayed.
The blood poured.
The Father heard.
The cup remained.

Sometime in the night, Judas arrived at Gethsemane, a garden he'd frequented with Jesus many times before (John 18:2). But this time, rather than joining the other disciples accompanying the Messiah, he arrived as the head of a thuggish mob armed with swords and clubs, dispatched by the "chief priests and elders of the people" (Matt. 26:47) to arrest Jesus and bring Him to heel.

Jesus stepped forward.
His enemies neared.
They tied Him, took Him.
His disciples fled.

It may surprise you to realize how quickly the next part of this story transpired. In no more than twelve hours, perhaps as few as nine (depending on how you reckon with the Bible's chronological terms), Jesus had been through two separate trials (each with three stages), had been declared guilty and sentenced to death, and was hanging on a cross. That's how hastily and unjustly the whole process was conducted. It was both rushed and renegade.

And biblically unlawful, even the trial overseen by Jewish legal experts.

The Jewish legal system, based on the law of Moses, was known for its commitment to justice. Deuteronomy 16, for example, gives these instructions to the people of Israel:

> Appoint judges and officials for your tribes in all your towns the LORD your God is giving you. They are to judge the people with righteous judgment. Do not deny justice or show partiality to anyone. . . . Pursue justice and justice alone. (vv. 18–20)

And yet, in the case of Jesus' trial by Jewish officials, justice was sacrificed on the altar of control and expedience. A mockery of justice, it failed to meet the minimum standards of Jewish law and custom, introducing one illegality and irregularity after another:

- *It was handled in private rather than public.* He was taken first for examination to Annas, the former high priest, who even in retirement continued to wield enormous influence. Then He was sent to Caiaphas, who was the current high priest and the son-in-law of Annas (John 18:13), not to mention having been the moving force behind the simmering plot to do away with Jesus (John 11:49–53). His sinister plan was now coming to full fruition, completely shielded from public view.
- *It happened in the middle of the night.* According to Jewish law, trials had to take place during daytime hours.
- *It happened hurriedly.* The entire trial was completed in less than a day, again contrary to Jewish law which stipulated that a case involving a capital offense could not be concluded until the following day, to allow opportunity for witnesses to be called. It

violated Old Testament laws requiring the defense to be thoroughly investigated. Instead, the leaders rushed to judgment to pronounce sentence as quickly as possible.

- *The judges were far from impartial.* Members of the Sanhedrin council—the Jewish governing body—were known enemies of Jesus. The officials who gathered for the emergency overnight session had reached their verdict before the defendant was ever presented for questioning; they were "looking for false testimony against Jesus so that they could put him to death" (Matt. 26:59). So when they began trotting out their procession of bogus witnesses, it really mattered little that "the testimonies did not agree" (Mark 14:56).

We were the ones who deserved to be tried, sentenced, and condemned to death. But when the holy Son of God stood on trial before this fraudulent kangaroo court, He stood there in our place, representing us, bearing our sins.

Nor did the presiding adjudicators attempt to hide their own predetermined feelings. Throughout the course of Jesus' trial, they spit on Him, slapped Him, blindfolded and beat Him, all while presumably giving Him His day in a court where "justice" would prevail.

To the minds of these authorities, Jesus simply could not be who He claimed to be—if He was, they'd surely know it. If the Messiah were here, they would be the first to recognize Him. And the Messiah they had long awaited surely wouldn't look, sound, and do things like the man in front of them looked and sounded and did.

Jesus was convicted
by His own people—
proclaimed guilty of blasphemy,
deserving of death—
all at the hands of lawbreakers.

And though they knew exactly what they were doing—breaking the law in their rush to judgment—Jesus also knew exactly what He was doing. He was offering up His life for the lawbreakers—"the righteous for the unrighteous, that he might bring [them] to God" (1 Peter 3:18). And His sacrifice was not just for those unrighteous religious leaders who tried and convicted Him unjustly; it was also for all those who, by breaking God's law, have set themselves against the One who came to save them.

Like you.
Like me.
Like them.
Like all of us.

We were the ones who deserved to be tried, sentenced, and condemned to death. But when the holy Son of God stood on trial before this fraudulent kangaroo court, He stood there in our place, representing us, bearing our sins.

At His first earthly trial, Jesus was judged unjustly at the hands of sinners. But one day the tables will be turned, and He will be the supreme Judge who will render righteous judgment to every unrepentant sinner.

In what sense do the actions of Jesus' accusers represent the entire human race's sinful treatment of Him, even those of us who are millennia and miles removed from His arrest and trial?

"Consider him who endured such hostility from sinners against himself, so that you won't grow weary and give up" (Heb. 12:3). How can meditating on the sufferings of Christ help you persevere in your battle against sin?

Lord Jesus, my love for You only deepens in seeing You so unfairly accused, so unjustly treated, with Your own law being broken as if broken over Your head. And yet You submitted to injustice because of Your love for lawbreakers. May I see my every sin as yet another assault against You, and may I never fail to be grateful for what You were willing to endure for the sake of sinners like me.

AMEN.

Day 24

Planned Developments

The Roman Trial of Christ

Again they shouted, "Crucify him!" Pilate said to them, "Why? What has he done wrong?" But they shouted all the more.

—MARK 15:13–14

What a headache of a way to start the day, Pilate must have thought. It wasn't even six o'clock in the morning. Yet here were the Jewish religious authorities on his doorstep demanding an audience, allegedly for the good of the empire.

The Sanhedrin, you understand, only possessed authority to deal with their partisan religious issues. As subjects of the Roman government, they could not carry out a public death sentence without getting the Romans to endorse and execute it. And at this point in time, such requests had to be cleared by Pontius Pilate, the designated governor in charge of first-century Judea.

But of what interest was a blasphemy complaint to a secular official who only cared about keeping peace in his territory? So the Jewish leaders, as a way of incentivizing Pilate to act on their case against Jesus, cast Him as a seditionist, an insurrectionist, a troublemaker leading a subversive rebellion against Caesar himself.

Now that was enough to open Pilate's ears. Any threat to Caesar was capable of getting the emperor's advocates out of bed in the morning. The Jewish priests and counselors had been right in their political calculations. They knew what they were doing.

Here, though, is what *we* need to know and remember:

> The kings of the earth take their stand,
> and the rulers conspire together
> against the LORD and his Anointed One. (Ps. 2:2)

And yet, as the prophet Daniel proclaimed to a pagan king, "Heaven rules!" (Dan. 4:26). Nothing happens anywhere on earth that God has not foreordained for His own wise reasons, for His redemptive purposes, for the ultimate good of His people. And for the eternal glory of His Son, Christ Jesus.

Could the Jewish leaders decide to hand Him over to Pilate? Yes, and they did. "We found this man misleading our nation," they claimed, "opposing payment of taxes to Caesar, and saying that he himself is the Messiah, a king" (Luke 23:2). But even with that charge, Pilate could "find no grounds for charging this man" (v. 4). So he made the Jewish leaders a deal.

God's plans cannot be thwarted. He will accomplish His righteous purposes even if the horrors of our times are the tools He employs.

Could they call Pilate's bluff and accept his offer to turn loose a violent felon in exchange for Jesus? Yes, and they did. In their rage they chose to act irrationally, even at the cost of endangering their community. "Release Barabbas to us!" they told Pilate, agreeing to the release of a man who "had been thrown into prison for a rebellion . . . and for murder" (Luke 23:18–19).

Could Pilate, frustrated, decide to pass Jesus along to another court? Yes, and he did. Discovering that Jesus was a Galilean, meaning He was technically under the jurisdiction of Herod Antipas, who (in God's providence) "happened" to be in Jerusalem at the time (Luke 23:7), Pilate lost no time in sending the prisoner on. Herod had sport with Jesus, posing absurd questions to Him and dressing Him in mock symbols of royalty. But he, too, declined to pass judgment.

Could Herod then decide to remand Him back to Pilate? Yes, and he did. But Pilate, unable to quell the raucous onlookers who'd been worked up by their leaders into a vengeful, bloodthirsty frenzy, "took some water, washed his hands in front of the crowd, and said, 'I am innocent of this man's blood. See to it yourselves!'" (Matt. 27:24).

Kill Him if you want. That was Pilate's final decision—or nondecision—to pass on the responsibility to a vicious crowd.

But only God—and His willing Son—could use this series of contemptible choices to help fulfill a plan He had put in place before the dawn of time. As Peter would later express in a public prayer,

> "Both Herod and Pontius Pilate, with the Gentiles and the people of Israel, assembled together against your holy servant Jesus, whom you anointed, to do whatever *your hand* and *your will* had predestined to take place." (Acts 4:27–28)

Do you see the importance of this? Not for one moment were any of the players in this travesty of justice the ultimate movers behind the action.

Were they guilty of spite and spinelessness? Yes.

Are we as guilty as they for our own selfish treatment of Jesus? Yes.

But underneath it all, His trial is another reminder that God's plans cannot be thwarted. Those who betrayed, tried, and condemned Jesus to death were guilty of treason against the Holy One of God. But they were fulfilling a plan that God had mercifully ordained so that they and treasonous sinners of every era could be pardoned and declared not guilty before Him.

Our world today is churning in vicious cycles of corruption and chaos. But no level of wickedness can have the final say because *Heaven rules.* God will accomplish His righteous purposes even if the horrors of our times are the tools He employs. And at the end of the day, "even human wrath will praise [Him]" (Ps. 76:10).

That's the key lesson from this whole insulting, infuriating spectacle of Jesus on trial. Evil actions carried out by malicious men actually became instruments in God's plan to rescue and redeem sinners from their sins. To rescue and redeem *us* from our sins. Such is the power of God to rule and overrule the most heinous schemes of the wicked.

Remembering Jesus standing before Herod, Pilate, and the Sanhedrin can comfort our souls when those in authority abuse their power, lie about us, and mistreat us. The same Jesus who endured being wrongly accused, incriminated, and violated can give us grace to bear up under unjust treatment.

As we faithfully follow Him, we can be sure He will always, ultimately lead us to the place of His choosing, regardless of what impediments may come against us along the way. We will never, ever find ourselves in a situation our God does not control.

What situations in your life or in today's world most challenge your confidence in God's ability to bring good out of evil?

How can realizing that no one's actions or decisions override His plans change your response to these situations?

Father in heaven, how I thank You for not allowing human selfishness and hatred to alter Your plan to pursue and redeem us. Thank You for the reminder that Heaven rules! May the example of Jesus encourage and strengthen me when I'm facing trials. And may my heart stay anchored to You in every hard place where I am required to walk.

AMEN.

Day 25

Steady as He Goes

The Majestic Silence of Christ

Like a lamb led to the slaughter
and like a sheep silent before her shearers,
he did not open his mouth.
—ISAIAH 53:7

Of the many incomparable qualities of Jesus, one of the most amazing to me is His ability to stay silent when falsely accused. His response differs so sharply from my own reflexive reactions when I feel unfairly attacked—and maybe yours as well. Subjected to blatant injustice, pinballed from one intolerable trial venue to the next, Jesus stands out more for what He *didn't* say than for what He *did* say.

Remarkable in His silence.

The "courtrooms" where He was tried, you understand, were not gaveled fortresses of decorum, with formal questioning and testimony volleyed back and forth in a stately, orderly fashion. Trials in these rogue settings were ruled not by fair play but by clamor and confusion, by belligerence and interruption. Most people in Jesus' position, far from *stifling* their voice, would've been *raising* it, pleading to be heard above the cacophony of competing sides.

Yet through it all He stood in the dock and said little. He absorbed the venom and held His peace.

- *With the Jewish leaders:* "'Don't you have an answer to what these men are testifying against you?' But he kept silent and would not answer" (Mark 14:60–61).

- *With Pilate:* "'Don't you hear how much they are testifying against you?' But he didn't answer him on even one charge" (Matt. 27:13–14).
- *With Herod:* "He kept asking him questions, but Jesus did not answer him" (Luke 23:9).

Back in Gethsemane, when the dark shadow of the cross loomed large before Him, He had poured out His heart to the Father—not just once but "a second time" (Matt. 26:42) and "a third time" (v. 44). He had prayed passionately and repeatedly for His Father to "let this cup pass from me" if there was any other way, any way possible, for Him to accomplish the work He had been sent to do (v. 39).

But once He emerged from the garden, Jesus laid His words aside. He left His prayers with heaven's Ruler, and He spoke only sparingly to everyone else from that point forward.

Again, note the contrast. How often, instead of talking with our heavenly Father about the trials we're undergoing, instead of wrestling to understand His purposes and perspectives, instead of bringing our hearts into alignment with His will, we vent our distress to everyone else. We dash off heated text messages and emails. We complain to anyone who will listen. We call out the motives and transgressions of others while painting ourselves in the best possible light.

Not Jesus. He didn't lash out. He didn't seek to disprove the lies that targeted Him. He didn't protest the unfairness of the proceedings nor make an appeal to a higher court. For the most part He remained silent. And the few times He did respond verbally, He spoke from neither fear nor self-vindication. While His accusers were consumed with rage, His temper never flared and His words were few, purposeful, and without sin.

Was He just being stoic? We've seen people who are sullen and angry in their silence. We've seen people steel themselves so as not to give their opponents the satisfaction of seeing them crack. But nothing in the demeanor of Christ comes across as tough or surly.

No doubt Jesus' silence was disconcerting to His interrogators. His unwillingness to answer their questions posed an unspoken challenge to their authority. Yet we see Him in Scripture not as a stoic, but as simply submitted to His Father, possessing a quiet confidence in His calling and in the truth of His identity.

Note that He never denied the truth by what He did or didn't say. But He chose not to return the barbs flung at Him or to defend Himself. Why? Because He "entrusted himself to the one who judges justly" (1 Peter 2:23). He knew the only one whose opinion really mattered would vindicate Him in due time. And He was willing to wait for God to act rather than lash out in an effort to prove His case before a human tribunal.

Though from a human perspective He might have seemed a victim, His silence made it clear that He was not, that these events were part of a divine plan He fully embraced. We see this in Gethsemane when He told Peter, "Put your sword away! Am I not to drink the cup the Father has given me?" (John 18:11). Note the quiet confidence, the clear statement of purpose. Jesus' life was in the hands of *God*, not those of His accusers or even His followers. He had no need for nor intention of defending Himself.

Jesus' silence fulfilled the Old Testament Messianic prophecy found in Isaiah's "song of the suffering servant":

> He was oppressed and afflicted,
> yet he did not open his mouth. (Isa. 53:7)

He meekly accepted the role of bearing His Father's verdict and judgment against our sin:

> All we like sheep have gone astray;
>   we have turned—every one—to his own way;
> and the LORD has laid on him
>   the iniquity of us all. (Isa. 53:6 ESV)

And this, I believe, is yet another reason for His silence—not just confidence in His own innocence, but the acceptance of our guilt. After all, isn't silence often an admission of wrongdoing? Someone accuses us of something, and we don't answer because there's something we don't want them to know. The reason we lower our heads, the reason we avoid eye contact, is that we know we are guilty as charged and that we deserve the resulting punishment.

Jesus, in this moment, in His silence, was standing in our place. He wasn't yet on the cross, though He would be soon enough. But He was already carrying the burden of our sin, being forced to answer for what we deserved to be charged with. The truth was on His side, but our sins were on His shoulders.

And our salvation was in His silence, the quiet, lamblike way He endured the punishment due us for our sins.

Today He is still mostly silent in the face of those who blaspheme Him—atheists who attack Him, critics who falsely accuse Him. But one day His voice will thunder loud and clear throughout all the earth. And all who have spoken against Him will be speechless before His majesty, power, and grace, while those who love and worship Him will sing eternal hallelujahs to the Lion of Judah.

What's your usual first reaction when you are falsely accused?

How might it be different if your first reaction was to go before God and lay your heart bare before Him?

Father, You put Your Son into a situation where He could not defend Himself without disowning me. The shame of my sin silenced His voice. But may the words He chose not to say in that moment resound in my continual witness—of You as my living God and of Your Son as my living Savior, whose sacrifice for me speaks volumes to my grateful heart.

AMEN.

Day 26

Covering the Cost

The Atoning Sacrifice of Christ

For the life of a creature is in the blood, and I have appointed it to you to make atonement on the altar for your lives, since it is the lifeblood that makes atonement.

—LEVITICUS 17:11

It's not easy for us as New Testament believers to get inside the minds of the Old Testament followers of Yahweh. They lived with the covenant promises made to Abraham and his descendants. They lived with the law handed down through Moses on Mount Sinai. They lived with the priestly structure and hierarchy that governed their worship habits—including, of course, the system of animal sacrifice God had put into place as their means of obtaining forgiveness for sin.

Though repetitive and costly, the regular rituals revealed His desire to restore fellowship with these repeat offenders He'd called to be His people. It provided them a way to be purified before Him.

At peace with Him.

Their sins atoned for.

The Hebrew words translated "atonement" and "make atonement" in the Old Testament carry the idea of covering—as in sins *covered*. This important word group, used some one hundred fifty times in the Old Testament, is linked with forgiveness of sin and the resulting reconciliation to God.

You've likely heard the noun form *kippur*, as in Yom Kippur, the traditional Jewish Day of Atonement. Established in Leviticus 16, this observance was prescribed as an annual ceremony in which the high priest entered into the Holiest Place in the temple and offered the blood of a young bull and a ram—a substitutionary sacrifice for his own sins as well as the sins of the people. "Atonement will be made for you on this day to cleanse you," the Bible says, "and you will be clean from all your sins before the LORD" (Lev. 16:30).

But looking back on those days from the other side of the cross, aren't you glad to be able to enjoy as accomplished fact what Old Testament believers could only anticipate by faith? All those elements of their worship—the blood, the sacrifice, the temple, the Holy Place—were symbols and shadows of a greater reality still to come. We have Jesus now, who "entered the most holy place once for all time, not by the blood of goats and calves, but by his own blood, having obtained eternal redemption" (Heb. 9:12). No longer are we required to come to the altar with our animal sacrifices—and keep coming, and keep coming, and keep coming, time after time, year after year—in order to secure atonement with our God.

Our atonement has come at great cost. None of our sins has simply been glossed over or ignored. Each of them has been paid for dearly. Each bears the red stain of Christ's blood.

We have something they didn't.

And yet maybe they had something *we* don't—or at least that we too easily forget. Maybe we need to be reminded that forgiveness *does* require sacrifice.

Think back again to those days of the Old Testament priesthood. As you read this description (one of many similar ones recorded in the book of Leviticus), underline or make a mental list of the different components and stages of the sacrificial system—starting with the sinful act and the recognition of guilt:

> "Now if any of the common people sins unintentionally by violating one of the LORD's commands, does what is prohibited, and incurs guilt, or if someone informs him about the sin he has committed, then he is to bring an unblemished female goat as his offering for the sin that he has committed. He is to lay his hand on the head of the sin offering and slaughter it at the place of the burnt offering. Then the priest is to take some of its blood with his finger and apply it to the horns of the altar of burnt offering. He is to pour out the rest of its blood at the base of the altar. . . . In this way the priest will make atonement on his behalf, and he will be forgiven." (Lev. 4:27–31)

Whew! What an onerous process. I for one am thrilled to be living on the "after Christ" side of history rather than "before Christ." I'm happy to know there will be no blood flowing from the altar at any of the church services I attend this year—or *any* year. I suspect you feel the same. But maybe it's helpful for you and me, as a reminder of Christ's sacrifice for our sins, to imagine waiting our turn at the scene of an Old Testament sacrifice.

Would our sin ever seem trivial to us, would it ever seem moderate in cost, if we were required to physically bring an animal sacrifice to the altar as a substitute to die in our place, for our sin? How vivid would the cost of our sin appear if forgiving it involved putting our guilty hand on the warm head of that innocent creature and hearing its cry of pain as the knife dug deep, as the blood gushed out, as its body fell limply to the ground at our feet? Would there be any question in our mind as to whether satisfying God's righteous justice came at the cost of great sacrifice?

And yet it does. For our every sin.

Store in your mind and heart four words that are always involved in atonement: *sin, sacrifice, substitute, satisfaction. Sin* requires a *sacrifice.* Jesus Christ, the sinless "Lamb of God" (John 1:29), was sacrificed as our *substitute.* And God's justice and righteous wrath were *satisfied.*

Hallelujah, we are forgiven! Hallelujah, our sins are covered! But this atonement has come at great cost. None of our sins has simply been glossed over or ignored. Each of them has been paid for dearly. Each bears the red stain of Christ's blood.

The only reason we're forgiven is that God accepts the price Jesus paid for us. To atone for us.

May we never, ever forget it.

What would be different about our present, our future, and how we relate to God if He had not made it possible for our sins to be atoned for?

As you've read this far, has God opened your eyes to see your need for a Savior and the price Jesus paid for your sin? If so, confess to Him that you are a sinner in need of forgiveness. Repent of (turn from) your sin. Place your faith in Christ and the sacrifice He made to satisfy the wrath of God. Thank Him that you will never experience His judgment because Jesus has made provision for your salvation.

Father, Your holiness is so intense and pure that I can never fully grasp it, and my sin is more evil and heinous than I can possibly comprehend. Were it not for Your mercy and the price paid by Jesus' precious blood, I would be utterly crushed by the weight of my sin. I am undone and offer up to You my unending gratitude and praise.

AMEN.

Day 27

Grand Central

The Atoning Work of Christ

He has appeared one time, at the end of the ages,
for the removal of sin by the sacrifice of himself.
—HEBREWS 9:26

What would you say is the greatest need all of humanity shares in common?

Some might suggest our need for food to eat and water to drink or, even more critically, for air to breathe. For sure, physical life cannot be sustained for any length of time without these basic necessities.

Others, mindful that we are more than physical beings, might say we have an even greater need for love. And certainly we cannot thrive without love, for we were made by God to live in loving relationship with Him and others.

However, God's Word reveals that because we are not only physical beings with souls, but also *sinners* from birth, our need for *forgiveness* is as great or greater than any other need we could possibly have.

Some time ago a woman wrote to me expressing a struggle that describes the predicament of the fallen human race: "I've gone through many battles trying to be good enough, trying to earn God's grace, and walking on eggshells, thinking God was going to throw me overboard if I did something wrong."

This woman *knows* she is a sinner in need of forgiveness, as are we all. Not only does sin place a burden of guilt and regret on us during our days here on earth; it also puts us at risk of forever being alienated from a holy God and subject to His eternal judgment. How fitting is it, therefore, that at this midway point of our journey through the life, work, and legacy of Jesus, we should come to the central message of the Bible.

Atonement.

You could say that our desperate need and God's gracious provision for our need lie at the crux of His plan for this world, for the word *crux* literally means "cross." And because this atoning work of Christ on the cross is indeed the core teaching of all the Scripture, it's not surprising that Scripture itself, from one end to the other, proclaims the grandness of this story far more effectively than I could possibly tell it. So rather than having you read more of my words today, I want to encourage you to read and ponder a series of selected passages from His Word.

If you're using this book during the season leading up to Easter, over the next couple of weeks you'll be joining Christians around the world in focusing on the sufferings and sacrifice of Christ on behalf of sinners. Regardless of when you're reading it, rather than scanning or skipping over these verses that may have been familiar to you since childhood (as I'm often tempted to do myself), take time to read them thoughtfully and prayerfully, perhaps even aloud. You may want to highlight words or phrases that describe (1) our sin problem and (2) what God has done to remedy our condition.

> Blessed is the God and Father of our Lord Jesus Christ, who has blessed us with every spiritual blessing in the heavens in Christ. For he chose us in him, before the foundation of the world, to be holy and blameless in love before him. He predestined us to be adopted as sons through Jesus Christ for himself, according to the good pleasure of his will. (Eph. 1:3–5)

> But we have sinned, and you were angry.
> How can we be saved if we remain in our sins?
> All of us have become like something unclean,

> and all our righteous acts are like a polluted garment;
> all of us wither like a leaf,
> and our iniquities carry us away like the wind. (Isa. 64:5–6)

"Truly I tell you, everyone who commits sin is a slave of sin." (John 8:34)

For whoever keeps the entire law, and yet stumbles at one point, is guilty of breaking it all. (James 2:10)

What a wretched man I am! Who will rescue me from this body of death? Thanks be to God through Jesus Christ our Lord! (Rom. 7:24–25)

Love consists in this: not that we have loved God, but that he loved us and sent his Son to be the atoning sacrifice for our sins. (1 John 4:10)

Christ redeemed us from the curse of the law by becoming a curse for us, because it is written, Cursed is everyone who is hung on a tree. (Gal. 3:13)

He himself bore our sins in his body on the tree; so that, having died to sins, we might live for righteousness. (1 Peter 2:24)

What the law could not do since it was weakened by the flesh, God did. He condemned sin in the flesh by sending His own Son in the likeness of sinful flesh as a sin offering. (Rom. 8:3)

> He was pierced for our transgressions;
> he was crushed for our iniquities;
> upon him was the chastisement that brought us peace,
> and with his wounds we are healed. (Isa. 53:5 ESV)

> For the wages of sin is death, but the gift of God is eternal life in Christ Jesus our Lord. (Rom. 6:23)

> He himself is the atoning sacrifice for our sins, and not only for ours, but also for those of the whole world. (1 John 2:2)

> Let whoever is wise pay attention to these things
> and consider the LORD's acts of faithful love. (Ps. 107:43)

Atonement. The etymology of this English word conveys the idea of unity and reconciliation—or as you may have heard it said, "at-one-ment." God has provided a way for estranged sinners to be forgiven from our enslaving sins and to be reconciled to Him, brought into harmony with Him, made one with Him.

All through the atoning work of Christ. Praise His name!

Why do you and I need the atoning work of Christ? How might you try explaining this to someone who has never heard or grasped the gospel?

What are some words or phrases you would use to describe an appropriate response to Christ's atoning work on our behalf?

Oh God, the enormity of Your redeeming love astounds me. Your initiative in sending Jesus to reconcile sinners to Yourself is a gift too grand to be treated lightly. I will never be able to fully fathom why You would cover me with Your righteousness, yet I am freed in Christ from ever doubting it. Please accept my humble, wholehearted gratitude for Your amazing grace.

AMEN.

Part Three

THE SEVEN LAST WORDS OF CHRIST

While the Savior hangs in indescribable torture on the cross,
let us listen to His dying words. . . .
His heart is still full of compassion and pity.
His voice is still uttering words of forgiveness and love
to the sinful and the wretched.
Oh, what affecting, consoling, and blessed words
fall from the lips of the Son of God
before He bows His head in death!

—David Harsha[23]

Day 28

Opening—and Closing—in Prayer

The Word of Forgiveness, Part 1

In return for my love they accuse me,
but I continue to pray.
—PSALM 109:4

Last words carry special significance. Even the quietest among us utter a lot of words throughout the course of our lives, many of them conveying little of lasting importance. But those who are given the opportunity to say something during their final hours don't typically comment on the weather or the alarming rise in gas prices. They talk about what matters most to them. They say things they want their loved ones to remember them by. They express what's on their hearts.

We see in that moment who they really are, unfiltered and unpretentious.

Scripture records seven statements Jesus made from the cross during those final six hours of suffering—His "last words" before His death and subsequent resurrection. Each of these statements provides insight into the richness and reality of the gospel as well as giving us an intimate gaze into the depths of His love for the Father and for the needy sinners He came to redeem.

Matthew Henry, one of my favorite old-time Bible commentators, makes an interesting observation about these last words. He wonders if perhaps "one reason why [Jesus] died the death of the cross was that he might have liberty of speech to the last, and so might glorify his Father, and edify those about him."[24] I do know that my life has never stopped being warmed, blessed, and comforted—truly edified—by these choice words from our Savior's lips, especially because they came while He was enduring a deeper, more intense form of agony than any other has ever known.

Jesus spoke . . . to the end. And we should listen.

His first utterance, spoken soon after He'd been nailed to the cross—or maybe while the nails were actively being driven—was not merely a statement. Notice the construction of this sentence:

> ***"Father, forgive them, because they do not know what they are doing."*** (Luke 23:34)

Do you see that this is a prayer? Jesus was speaking to His Father.

You'll remember that Jesus began His public ministry praying. He prayed while standing in the waters of His baptism, and "heaven opened" above Him (Luke 3:21), bringing the voice of the Father affirming His love for the Son.

Prayer, of course, remained the pattern of Christ's life after that. He prayed in the mornings and into the night. He prayed in secret and in public. He prayed to His Father incessantly.

It's only natural then—if anything was natural about Jesus' crucifixion—that here at the end of His earthly ministry He would continue this lifelong (indeed, eternal) conversation with the Father. He was no longer in a position to heal or teach or place His hands on the tired shoulders of the hurting and bereaved. But He could pray. Nothing—*nothing!*—could stop His praying.

They could make Him walk the long path to this place called "The Skull"—*Calvary* in Latin, *Golgotha* in Hebrew—even as the pain of each staggering step shot upward like daggers through His throbbing legs.

They could stake His bleeding body to a heavy, wooden, torturous device of death, hammering the nails through the tender flesh and cartilage of His feet and hands. They could jolt His cross upright alongside those of two criminals, "one on the right and one on the left" (Luke 23:33).

But they could not stop His praying.

Historians tell us that death by crucifixion was one of the cruelest ways a person could be executed. Not only was this the mode of punishment the Father chose for Jesus, but it followed a brutal gauntlet of harsh beatings and floggings, with reeds whipped like fiery switches against His body and a woven crown of thorns plunged into His scalp. On top of that came the mocking, the ridicule, the angry derision. Who could have blamed Jesus if He had joined the ranks of crucifixion victims who were known to scream curses at their Roman executioners, sometimes having their tongues cut out to quiet them.

Jesus was no longer in a position to heal or teach or place His hands on the tired shoulders of the hurting and bereaved. But He could pray. Nothing—*nothing!*—could stop His praying.

Yet Jesus didn't curse.

Instead, He prayed.

I think of individuals I've known who have come to a point where they can't be as active as they once were. They may be confined to their homes, even to their beds, restricted by physical limitations or discomfort from doing things that feel purposeful and productive to them. They can't get involved in a lot of ministry tasks anymore. Their stamina won't hold out long enough for them to serve in ways that they equate with bringing real help and cheer to others.

But they can pray—and they do. In God's economy, their prayers may be the most important ministry of their lives.

Tomorrow we'll consider *what* our Savior prayed in this holy moment. But while we contemplate today this first word spoken from the cross, marvel that at the end of His earthly life Jesus prayed to His

Father, pleading with Him on behalf of undeserving sinners. And see in your own prayers a ministry that attracts the Father's ear and results in mercy being sent from heaven to earth. Never allow yourself to wonder whether prayer has any impact or whether it can connect people to the outpoured blessings of God.

Christ's first word from the cross reminds us that our prayers can make an eternal difference, no matter where and when we offer them up.

What are the biggest obstacles you face in developing and maintaining a lifestyle of prayerfulness?

Think of how people brutalized Jesus physically and verbally as He was being crucified. And yet His first word was to His Father, not to His tormentors. Is there a situation you are facing that calls for you to follow His example?

Our Father, thank You for opening to us the portal of prayer, for desiring ongoing fellowship with us, for the privilege of calling out to You and blessing others through prayer. Help me cultivate this lifestyle of prayer even in my most trying and limited circumstances, interceding for others as Your Son interceded for us.

AMEN.

Day 29

Interceding for Transgressors

The Word of Forgiveness, Part 2

He bore the sin of many
and interceded for the rebels.
—ISAIAH 53:12

Back in simpler times, before the cross was on the mind of anyone but Jesus, when a day with Him might include sitting out on a sunny patch of ground somewhere, amazed at the freshness and richness of His teaching, He had said something astonishing:

> "You have heard that it was said, Love your neighbor and hate your enemy. But I tell you, love your enemies and pray for those who persecute you." (Matt. 5:43–44)

Profound in theory, some listeners must have thought, *but counterintuitive to real life.* Others may have found the idea too radical or simply impossible to live out in practice, even when it came from Someone as uniquely impressive as Jesus.

"Love your enemies." Was Jesus just *saying* that? Or was He prepared to *do* it?

His first word from the cross is all the answer we need.

"Father, forgive them . . ." (Luke 23:34)

"Them" included a detachment of Roman soldiers who'd been dutifully, perhaps delightedly, abusing Jesus with flesh-lacerating weapons and other sharp objects. It included officials like Pontius Pilate and Herod Antipas, who had fecklessly refused to protect an innocent Man. It included members of a wild, fickle, feverish mob chanting for His blood. It even included disciples He'd chosen and befriended, whom He'd traveled with and poured His life into, who'd now escaped into hiding.

And of course, "forgive them" includes you and me. In answer to the haunting question from the timeless spiritual, "Were You There When They Crucified My Lord?"—yes, yes, we were. We were there with all the hostile persecutors and spineless runaways who did nothing to prevent Jesus' murder—who, in fact, did everything to push Him there.

"Father, forgive them, because they do not know what they are doing." (v. 34)

But *He* did. He knew exactly what He was doing.

Jesus was always acutely aware that His actions were fulfilling Old Testament prophecy. And He knew the prophet Isaiah had foretold that the Messiah would make intercession "for the rebels" (Isa. 53:12)—"for the transgressors" (ESV). Because He was indeed the Messiah, interceding for transgressors and rebels was part of His divinely appointed ministry. And nowhere were human transgression and rebellion more manifest in His lifetime than here at Golgotha, on this historic crossroads of a day on the calendar.

Jesus also knew He was there to participate with His Father in being the answer to His own prayer. If you ever find yourself speaking with someone who has reduced Jesus into being merely a good teacher, an admirable role model—meek and mild and nothing more—consider taking them to this place, on this day, where He spoke these breathtaking words of forgiveness. Because when He prayed, "Father, forgive them," He was essentially saying, "Father, punish *Me* for their sins."

Forgive *them.* Forsake *Me.*

Let *Me* be the sacrifice. Let *them* go free. Plunge all their sins into the depths of the sea.

That's not soft and gentle; that's gutsy and heroic. That's the heart of the One whose desire that we be forgiven moved Him to give His life for us.

To many, of course, His words will only be words. They still don't "know what they are doing," even as was once the case with us. Yet ignorance is not innocence. Spiritual blindness results from unbelief and rebellion, so it is just one more piece of damning evidence of our guilt and depravity.

Until God opens our eyes, we don't realize—we can't realize—the heinous nature of our sin, how God views it, what it did to Jesus. For the "god of this age has blinded the minds of the unbelievers" (2 Cor. 4:4).

Yet in spite of our sin and our blindness toward it, Christ's heart toward you and me is one of forgiveness. Long before we knew who He was or the crushing, treacherous enormity of our rebellion, He prayed for our pardon. He also paid the price that made it possible for a holy, just God to pardon sinners and release them from their debt. He shed His blood—as our Substitute—so we could be forgiven. And to this day, Jesus is the sinner's Advocate, pleading our case before the Father and offering His shed blood to satisfy the Father's righteous anger and judgment against our sin.

When Jesus prayed, "Father, forgive them," He was essentially saying, "Father, punish *Me* for their sins." Forgive *them*. Forsake *Me*. Let *Me* be the sacrifice. Let *them* go free.

Surely this calls for faith, repentance, and eternal wonder and gratitude on our part. And it calls for even more. You see, the cross of Christ not only provides pardon for our offenses against a holy God. It also moves and enables us to pray for and extend forgiveness to those who have sinned against *us*. To love our enemies as He loved us when we were His enemies.

I know it's a lot to ask. Forgiveness is hard to do. Perhaps you'd say it's *more* than you can do. But none of us, hearing Christ's words of forgiveness, can ever say He doesn't understand how deeply, gravely, personally we've been wronged. And none of us who claim to follow Him can ignore His call to forgive those who have wronged us.

Jesus prayed for the vilest, the most depraved, of His enemies to be pardoned. That means there is no one outside the reach of His love and mercy—not you, and not anyone who has wronged you. No one has sinned so greatly that He does not want them to be forgiven.

Remember, our sin was unforgivable, too, until Jesus prayed what He prayed and did what He did on the cross to make that forgiveness possible!

Loving and forgiving His enemies, just as He taught us to do.

How can Jesus' prayer for His enemies to be forgiven help you when you feel burdened by the weight of your sins?

Is there someone who has sinned against you and stands in need of God's forgiveness? Would you stop in this moment and make Jesus' prayer your prayer?

Father, thank You for a Savior who cared more about my receiving forgiveness than He cared about His own life and who chose to meet my need even when I didn't know I had it. Give me grace to extend to others the forgiveness I have received from You, so they can come to know You and be fully forgiven through Christ's sacrifice on their behalf.

AMEN.

Day 30

The Gift of Faith

The Word of Assurance, Part 1

Two others—criminals—were also led away
to be executed with him.

—LUKE 23:32

Where does faith come from?

In some ways it's a mystery. Faith is something *God* does, something *God* gives, more than it's something *we* do—which means that saving faith is a sovereign work, a gift of God. "No one can come to me," Jesus said, "unless the Father who sent me draws him. . . . No one can come to me unless it is granted to him by the Father" (John 6:44, 65).

At the same time, faith is profoundly intimate and personal. God doesn't perform this work from a detached, mystical distance but by actively involving Himself in a person's life. He somehow imprints His presence around them in such a way that they are awakened to Him, take notice of Him, and open their hearts to what He is making known about Himself and about them.

Faith, in other words, is complex and hard to understand, yet it's also simple and hard to miss once God opens blind eyes and imparts this gift to unbelieving hearts. And that miraculous, life-altering gift of faith is right here to see, plain as day, at the cross of Christ.

For His execution, the Bible tells us, Jesus was positioned directly between two robbers. We don't know the specific crimes either one had committed; in fact, we know nothing about their backstories. We only know they each had contempt for Jesus, that "in the same way" as the casual bystanders and gloating conspirators on the ground, "even the criminals who were crucified with him taunted him" (Matt. 27:44). In their dying hours they were deriding the only One who could give them life.

But then something happened, something utterly unexplainable apart from the intervening grace of God.

One of these two criminals had a sudden change of heart.

What could possibly trigger such an abrupt turn of mind? Maybe it had something to do with the mocking sign the executioners had crudely lettered at Pilate's orders and tacked above Jesus' head: "This is Jesus, the King of the Jews" (Matt. 27:37). Or maybe it was the fact that Jesus didn't rage at His tormentors but rather prayed for them—for their forgiveness!—even as His body screamed with pain above the angry, jeering crowd.

Where God is at work, there is always a way.

Or maybe, ironically, it was the cries of the hecklers themselves, shouting, "He saved others, but he cannot save himself!" (Mark 15:31). *What do you mean He's "saved others"? He can save people? Could He save me? Who* is *this person they call Jesus?*

All we know for sure is that one of these violent criminals, who moments earlier had been belittling and blaspheming the dying Man at his side, redirected his attention to the thief two crosses over and rasped out a biting rebuke, coming hard to Jesus' defense:

> "Don't you even fear God, since you are undergoing the same punishment? We are punished justly, because we're getting back what we deserve for the things we did, but this man has done nothing wrong." Then he said, "Jesus, remember me when you come into your kingdom." (Luke 23:40–42)

Don't look now, but I think we just heard the gospel.

Now, we have no reason to believe that this condemned criminal had ever been a student of theology or that he was even remotely familiar with religious concepts. And yet his words, I dare say, will preach.

- *He realized God was to be feared,* that a vast chasm existed between the created and the Creator.
- *He realized that he was guilty,* that he had sinned against this God to whom we all are accountable and that he deserved to be condemned to death.
- *He realized Jesus was innocent,* that He was dying a death He did not deserve.
- *He realized Jesus was a King with a kingdom* and that his only hope for the next life was to appeal to this King for mercy and a royal pardon.

I have no explanation for how a hardened criminal could know any of these things except that God is able to penetrate the hardest of hearts and give them the gift of repentance and faith. In fact, not one of us who has received Christ has come to Him any other way. Everything this convicted thief said of himself is true of you and of me.

- We have sinned.
- We deserve to be eternally separated from God in hell.
- We are helpless to save ourselves.
- We need a Savior.

What could either of these criminals do to change their lives, now that they were under a death sentence and currently in the act of being executed? There was no undoing or making up for the things they'd done. But where God is at work, there is always a way. Anyone anywhere can receive the gift of faith and can suddenly, no matter how unexpectedly, see "the light of the knowledge of the glory of God in the face of Jesus Christ" (2 Cor. 4:6 ESV).

Based on Scripture, how would you describe your life and the condition of your heart before you came to faith in Jesus Christ? What did you have in common with the thief on the cross?

What's your "faith story"? Whether you were a child or further along in life, what do you recall about how God made Himself known to you, showed you your spiritual need, and gave you faith to believe the gospel and turn to Christ for salvation? Who might be blessed or helped by hearing you share that story?

Oh Father, thank You for this amazing testimony of how You supernaturally granted faith to the condemned criminal who hung beside Your Son on the cross. How grateful I am for Your gift of faith. Thank You for seeking me and finding me and leading me home to You. Use my life, Lord—my words and my encounters—as a means through which You can bring saving faith to those You put in my path.

AMEN.

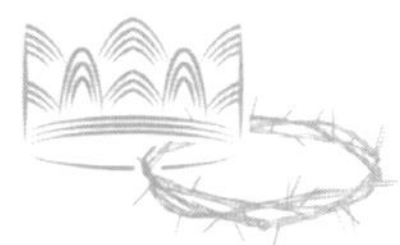

Day 31

No Doubt

The Word of Assurance, Part 2

"Truly I tell you, today you will be with me in paradise."
—LUKE 23:43

Some time ago I talked with a woman whose dad had recently died. Both her parents had been longtime believers in Christ. But now her grief-stricken mom was being plagued with gnawing doubt, asking over and over again: "Do you really think he's in heaven?"

Perhaps you are among the many who struggle at times with doubts or fears over what happens to us and others after death. *Have I [they] been good enough . . . faithful enough . . . to get into heaven? How can I be sure?*

Jesus' first word from the cross was a prayer for pardon of His enemies. His second statement was a word of assurance to a dying man who had no human reason to hope he would ever be welcome in heaven. This word can settle all doubts for every sinner who has come to Christ for mercy.

Scripture affirms that it is in the heart of God to save rather than condemn sinners. We see that heart in His message to the prophet Ezekiel: "Do I take any pleasure in the death of the wicked? . . . Instead, don't I take pleasure when he turns from his ways and lives?" (Ezek. 18:23).

But what about all the sins we've committed? What about our faults and flaws? Our halfhearted devotion to Jesus? How can we expect Him to welcome us when we stand before Him on the other side?

When the repentant thief turned his face toward Jesus and asked Him to "remember me," think of all the things that Jesus, being God, could "remember" about how this man had chosen to live his life. The convicted criminal was right: he was being "punished justly" (Luke 23:41). Death was a fitting payback for the many evils he'd committed. And yet Jesus said to him,

"Truly I tell you, today you will be with me in paradise."

Astonishing. See how quick He is to speak words of assurance to those who come to Him with a humble, contrite heart. This man who deserved nothing but rejection and judgment got nothing but mercy and grace.

There's something else I find stunning about this statement by Jesus. It's the same promise Jesus had made just the night before to His closest friends, the men who'd shared life with Him through almost all His earthly ministry. During their last meal together, He'd told them about His "Father's house" and its "many rooms" and about how He was going to "to prepare a place for" them. Then He'd added, "I will come again and take you to myself, so that where I am you may be also" (John 14:2–3).

How magnificently generous of Jesus. Yet who else in His life, if not these disciples, would make more sense as His invited guests? What a glorious reward to share with friends who had demonstrated, even imperfectly, their love and devotion toward Him.

But surely the thief on the cross was a different matter. What could possibly make the Father's house a suitable home for a man Jesus had never laid eyes on before the day of His death, a man who'd arguably never done anything holy in his whole life, a man who just minutes before had mocked and derided Him?

There's only one answer to that question: the open arms of Jesus to the repentant heart.

"No one who comes to me will ever be hungry. . . . The one who comes to me I will never cast out. . . . This is the will of my Father: that everyone who sees the Son and believes in him will have eternal life, and I will raise him up on the last day" (John 6:35, 37, 40).

In other words, don't *ever* think that He (or the Father) will reject your repentant heart or that your faith will be unrewarded. Don't *ever* imagine Him barricading His forgiveness behind a series of hoops for you to jump through or a list of fifteen tasks for you to accomplish as proof that He should take you seriously.

Jesus is *quick* to save. He is *eager* to forgive. He did not die so He could raise the bar on His mercy, but rather so He could lower it to the least likely of sinners who come seeking hope and life through Him.

Jesus is *quick* to save. He is *eager* to forgive. He did not die so He could raise the bar on His mercy, but rather so He could lower it to the least likely of sinners who come seeking hope and life through Him.

This "word of assurance" from Christ is a foundational truth on which to build unshakable confidence and hope. It not only changed one man's life and his entire eternal future; it will also change the way you and I approach the Father through the Son. It means we are welcome. It means we are wanted. It means He hears and responds to us when we look to Him as our only source of help and salvation.

It also should change forever the way we view death—both our own death and that of our friends, family, and loved ones. Those who die in the Lord can look forward to "paradise"—an eternity of peace and happiness with Him, promised to those who give up the futile pursuit of earning their own righteousness and by faith accept Christ's righteousness as their own. To put it in Paul's words, "to be absent from the body" is "to be present with the Lord" (2 Cor. 5:8 NKJV).

At the end of the day our eternal destiny is based on simple trust—*"Jesus, remember me"*—and on His mercy and grace—*"Today you will be with me in paradise."*

Not because of how much we know, how hard we've tried, or how much good we've done for Him. But because we have believed and received what *He* has done for us.

The psalmist reminds us that

> The sacrifice pleasing to God is a broken spirit.
> [He] will not despise a broken and humbled heart. (Ps. 51:17)

All we need to do is repent. Believe. And for the rest of your life, repeat as necessary, perpetually offering to Him the sacrifice of a humble heart. Christ has died so you can be with Him in paradise. Experience the peace of that promise this moment. Today.

What faulty assumptions about God are at the heart of doubting His mercy and forgiveness?

Who might you need to encourage with the knowledge that those who turn to Jesus for salvation will never be turned away from heaven?

Thank You, Lord, for saving the thief on the cross and for including this incident in Scripture as an encouragement, reminding us that no one is ever more than a single breath away from receiving Your forgiveness and experiencing life with You forever. Thank You for the assurance that You delight to save all those who come to You for mercy.

AMEN.

Day 32

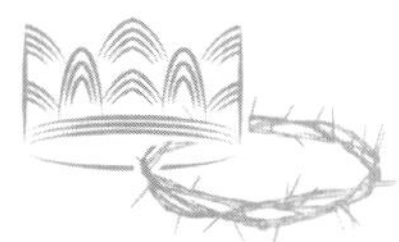

Comprehensive Coverage

The Word of Devotion, Part 1

Cast your burden on the LORD,
and he will sustain you.
—PSALM 55:22

The first three words Jesus spoke from the cross reveal His heart's desire for others.

First, remember, He prayed to His Father, asking forgiveness for His tormentors.

Second, He assured the repentant thief, "Today you will be with me in paradise" (Luke 23:43).

Then, third, He spoke to his mom.

Mary, of course, is most familiar to us from the events surrounding Jesus' birth. How often we've marveled at her humble, surrendered, worshipful response to the angel's announcement that she would carry the Son of God. And we remember how later, after the shepherds had paid their visit to baby Jesus in the manger, Mary "treasured up all these things, pondering them in her heart" (Luke 2:19 ESV). Though the events of Jesus' birth were surely difficult, our general impression of her from the Christmas story is one of beauty and peace, of comfort and joy.

But then came those haunting, troubling words spoken to Mary when she and Joseph took Jesus to be dedicated in the temple. As the aged Simeon took the infant into his arms that day, he'd prophesied over Mary: "A sword will pierce your own soul" (Luke 2:35). And now, decades later, at the foot of her beloved Son's cross, that painful "sword" must have sunk in deeply, nearly cutting her heart in two.

There she stood. That's all the Bible says about her presence, that she was "standing by the cross of Jesus" (John 19:25). Around her, there at His feet where everyone could see and hear, the soldiers who'd carried out His crucifixion raucously gambled with one another for His clothing. Yet Jesus, suffering not only the indignity of public nakedness but the intensity of wracking pain, used some of His few remaining words to express care and concern for His mother.

Jesus died not only to absorb the penalty of our sin and to save our souls from the wrath of God but also to redeem everything that is broken and isolating and incomplete in our fractured, dysfunctional world.

When you and I look at the cross, we tend to focus—as we should—on its spiritual implications. Jesus' prayer that others be forgiven. His promise of paradise to the dying criminal. The sacrifice He paid for us, the substitute He willingly became for us.

But His word to Mary from the cross tells us that His care and concern for His own reaches into every sphere of our lives, not just the spiritual. Jesus died not only to absorb the penalty of our sin and to save our souls from the wrath of God but also to redeem everything that is broken and isolating and incomplete in our fractured, dysfunctional world.

We have a Savior who cares about all that concerns us.

We see this so clearly in this moment at the cross. Here was Jesus, centrally engaged in performing the most important work ever accomplished in the history of the world. He had just six hours in which to secure our salvation. Six hours out of all the accumulated hours spread out across the millennia of human existence. Yet to what—and to whom—did He allot a portion of that small handful of hours?

"Jesus saw his mother and the disciple he loved standing there" (John 19:26).

Imagine the fears that must have gripped Mary's heart in those hours. Reading between the lines of Scripture, it seems likely that her husband, Joseph, had died years earlier, in which case the responsibility for her provision and care would have fallen on Jesus as the firstborn son. We know she had younger children who didn't yet believe Jesus' claims about Himself. Presumably she also had acquaintances—both Jewish and Roman—who knew of her loyalty to this one they despised and had judged to be a criminal. How long before her motherly courage to stand here at His cross might subject her to even crueler scrutiny?

Would she be safe? Would she be cared for? How would her daily, practical needs be met? What would everyday life look like for Mary once Jesus was gone?

Jesus was mindful of those questions. He cared about what she would face in the days ahead. He cared about *her*. And He showed His care in a practical way, by making loving, adequate provision for her through John, the beloved disciple, who was standing with Mary at the cross.[25]

He said to his mother,

"Woman, here is your son."

Then he said to the disciple,

"Here is your mother." (John 19:26–27)

In the midst of carrying out the most important work in the history of the world, Jesus did not overlook what others might have considered a relatively insignificant task—tending to the future needs of His mother. And He took pains to entrust her to the care of someone even closer than a natural son. Someone He knew who would share her faith and her love for Him. Who would love and honor the one who had loved and honored Him for all of His earthly life. Who would protect her, provide for her, and meet her needs when He was no longer physically present with her.

"I will not leave you comfortless," Jesus had promised His closest friends as the time drew near for Him to die and depart from this earth (John 14:18 KJV). Now, as a loving son, He said the same to His mother. And He says the same to you.

When you are removed from sources of provision you've counted on, from comforts you've longed for, you can be sure that Jesus will always, always provide what you need for each season of your life.

Everything you lack, everything you need, everything you yearn for, He knows about—and cares about. He will care for you.

From the cross, all the way to where you are.

In what areas or seasons of your life have you sometimes felt cut off from Christ's care and attention? How does Jesus' devotion to His mother comfort and reassure your heart?

How does tending to the practical needs of family members He has entrusted to your care glorify God and make the gospel believable?

Jesus, Your tender, thoughtful care for those You love amazes me. Thank You for assuming responsibility for every area of our lives, for the way You arrange and attend to the smallest needs and details, and for the assurance that there will never be a time when we will not be provided for. May I not neglect or resent caring for those for whom I am responsible.

AMEN.

Day 33

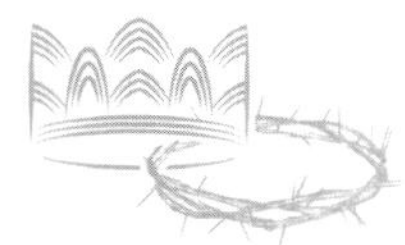

Family Connections

The Word of Devotion, Part 2

"Whoever does the will of my Father in heaven
is my brother and sister and mother."
—MATTHEW 12:50

Clustered around the cross that dark day, in stark contrast to the angry, restless mob, stood a handful of onlookers whose hearts were broken and whose eyes were fixed on the Man suspended in the middle, dying between two convicted criminals.

Mary, the mother of Jesus, was there. Her sister was present too. Most commentators, piecing together the various Gospel accounts, believe this woman's name was Salome, the wife of Zebedee and the mother of two of Christ's disciples, James and John.

Scripture refers to two other women present that day, each named Mary as well. Mary, the wife of Clopas, was perhaps the mother of another apostle. And then there was Mary Magdalene, whom Jesus had delivered from a tangle of "seven demons" (Luke 8:2) and who had become one of His faithful, long-term followers. Rounding out the group was John—"the disciple [Jesus] loved" (John 19:26)—who at first had fled in fear with the other members of Christ's inner circle but had dared to return and stand vigil with the others.

So Jesus had family around Him—but more than family. For even those not related by blood were connected by something more powerful, more magnetic, than mere biology and bloodlines. The one factor that held this group together so closely was the Man whose blood now dripped from His hands and feet and side, seeping down the cross and staining the ground beneath them.

Their love, faith, and belief in Jesus was what made these witnesses truly one.

Truly family.

This was the united body—the shared family of believers—that Jesus was giving His life to create. This new family created at the cross does not exclude the kindred attachments of birth families or give us leave to ignore their needs. Rather, it multiplies and transforms our natural family relationships, broadening them into a brotherhood and sisterhood that keeps *anyone* from being abandoned or neglected, from being orphaned or widowed, bereft or invisible.

Distance can intrude, death can intervene, selfish choices can interrupt, hard circumstances can inconvenience. But wherever those who belong to Jesus might be, touched by any situation in life, there are other members of His extended family who can embrace them, minister to their needs, and provide the companionship of a common heartbeat, passion, and purpose.

So when Jesus lowered His eyes, catching sight of the familiar faces staring up at Him, family was the lens through which He viewed their distraught expressions. Then He made the connection explicit:

To His mother: ***"Woman, here is your son."***
To John, His beloved disciple: ***"Here is your mother."***
(John 19:26–27)

"Woman." To our modern ears, this way of addressing His mother might sound cold. But Jesus certainly communicated no disrespect or lack of love to the woman who had given birth to Him. Perhaps He avoided addressing her with the more familiar "Mother" to keep us from being tempted to exalt Mary beyond what was appropriate. But the less sentimental language also hints at new family lines He was drawing—and He was drawing all His people inside those lines.

Jesus was deliberately establishing in their minds (and leaving clear instructions for us as well) that a new set of primary relationships, stronger than blood ties, now existed in His kingdom. Within the interconnectedness of His spiritual family, each of us—whoever we are—has the most in common with those people whose faith in Christ intersects our own.

In other words, our most valuable kinships in life are forged at the cross, formed around our mutual relationship with Jesus, and are literally built to last forever. The responsibilities we rightly owe to our physical families in love and obedience to Christ extend beyond these people as well. We as believers have an even wider call to care for and minister to our brothers and sisters in Christ and to live with the grateful confidence that they, too, will care for us.

Our most valuable kinships in life are forged at the cross, formed around our mutual relationship with Jesus, and are literally built to last forever.

We are together in Him. We are one. We are family.

So even though John was not Mary's naturally born son, he picked up on Jesus' dying, divine directive. "From that hour," the gospel reports, "the disciple took her into his home" (John 19:27).

How grateful I am for spiritual brothers and sisters, mothers and fathers, families, who have taken me under their wings and into their hearts and homes over the years, particularly in the decades I spent as a single woman, providing friendship, encouragement, practical counsel, and assistance. And what a joy it has been to open my heart and home to others, to care for them, assure them of His love, and come alongside them in times of discouragement or need.

Christ calls us to be His family here on earth. And it all came—it all *comes*—from the thoughtful care and devotion Christ initiated in the midst of the pain and peril of the cross. The family bond that He desires for us and desires the world to see *in* us is too big and broad to be confined to the handful of people we share a name and some DNA with. We have been gathered and adopted into a worldwide, multigenerational family that only the power and blood of Christ could create.

Our job is to love our brothers and sisters in Christ.

Our privilege is to be loved by them.

If you're hesitant to reach out to others from among God's people for practical help, prayer, and guidance, what might be causing you to hold back?

Who might God's Spirit be opening your eyes to notice—someone who needs the care of your shared family connection in Christ?

Our Father, what a marvel this is. You've formed Your people into a family, and You've invited me to be part of it. Help me to love and be devoted to Your children the way Christ has devoted Himself to us and has instructed us to care for others. Thank You for these brothers and sisters You've given me. May we honor You and Your Son by loving each other well.

AMEN.

Day 34

Why?

The Word of Dereliction, Part 1

Why are you so far from saving me,
from the words of my groaning?
—PSALM 22:1 ESV

Nine a.m.[26]

During the first three hours He hung on the cross, He broke the silence three times. He prayed for forgiveness for His enemies, assured the penitent thief that he would be with Him in paradise, and provided for the care of His mother.

Twelve noon.

Suddenly, just as the sun was at its highest point in the sky, pitch-black darkness descended on the land, dramatically and visibly representing the divine judgment that fell upon Jesus during this most painful, difficult phase of His redeeming work.

Jesus had already suffered cruelly at the hands of humans. Now, during the three long hours before His final breath, the Light of the World was plunged into a deep, unfathomable darkness of body and soul.

Three p.m.

During the Passover week, priests in the temple had been plunging knives into perhaps hundreds of thousands of sacrificial Passover lambs, the blood flowing from the altar, down a steep ravine, and draining through a channel into the Kidron Valley.[27] And now, on the hill of Golgotha nearby, the Passover Lamb of God (1 Cor. 5:7) was dying for the sins of the world. The rising tide of His agony and suffering had reached flood-crest stage. As the prophet Joel foretold, the sun had faded to black, and Christ Jesus would now

> roar from Zion
> and make his voice heard from Jerusalem. (Joel 3:15–16)

During those hours before noon, Jesus had cried out on behalf of the souls and needs of those around Him. Now, hidden from sight behind the black veil of excruciating darkness, Jesus cried out to God about His own anguish of soul.

"My God, my God, why have you forsaken me?" (Matt. 27:46 ESV)

There is no way we can fully fathom the depth and meaning contained in these words.

You see, Jesus had never, ever been separated from His Father. Imagine that. He had always done God's will. Guilt and shame had never cut Him off from being welcome in the Father's presence. The cross He'd carried for much of His lifetime—being reviled, rejected, abandoned, and misunderstood by others—had been more demeaning and devastating than any of us has ever known. And yet He'd always known—had *perfectly* known—that the Father was His dependable refuge and would never, ever push Him away.

Until now.

Until this staggering moment of alienation and abandonment.

Elizabeth Barrett Browning poetically referred to this breathless appeal of Christ as "Immanuel's orphaned cry."[28]

We often focus on the physiological and psychological aspects of what Jesus suffered. But keep in mind that crucifixion, though horrifically cruel and archaic to our senses, was actually quite common in the Roman era. Thousands upon thousands were put to death by this gruesome form of capital punishment. So while there's no discounting the horrendous pain Jesus endured by being nailed to a wooden cross,

He was hardly the only person to experience such agony. What we mustn't lose sight of is the fact that this physical suffering was minuscule compared to His *spiritual* suffering—the separation from His Father, the breach in their fellowship.

Jesus had been forsaken by His fellow humans. He had even been abandoned by His disciples. But never before had His Father been far from Him, turned a deaf ear to Him, or—even worse—actively caused His pain.

You may have heard it said that God in heaven turned His face away from His Son on the cross. This could make us imagine that God was only passively engaged in the judgment of Christ for our sin. But let's be careful about sanitizing our version of events to make it sound any more palatable or less severe than it actually was.

As difficult as our minds find this reality to be, Scripture tells us that "the LORD was pleased to crush him" (Isa. 53:10). The Father placed on Jesus the curse we deserved for our sin (see Gal. 3:10–13). God was actively, intentionally, directly involved in imputing our sin to His Son (see 2 Cor. 5:21).

The Father did this.

Jesus' Father did this.

So hear Christ's cry again now in all its horror and heartbreak:

"My God, my God, why have you forsaken me?"

"The word of dereliction," Oswald Sanders called this agonizing sentence. The cry of the Son's utter abandonment by His Father as He took all our sin on Himself.

Though their hands carried out the horrible crime, ultimately it was neither the Jews nor the Romans who put Jesus to death. The Father put His own Son to death. God turned His full anger against Jesus, raining down an eternity's worth of condemnation on this One who was made "to be sin for us" (2 Cor. 5:21).

On this sacred, sacrificial Lamb.

Yes, it "pleased" the Lord to do this—that is, it fulfilled His purpose to carry out divine justice in this fashion. And yet, at the same time, *He could not have been more pleased with His Son*. Saving us from our sin is what Jesus had come to earth to do, and He had done just that. He had stayed true to His mission. Even in being assailed by His Father, facing the ultimate test of faith, He had responded with the ultimate expression of trust and obedience. He'd done exactly what His Father had sent Him to accomplish.

Jesus' suffering on the cross was not "divine child abuse," as some detractors have labeled it. He *willingly* bore the wrath of God out of love for the Father and love for us, knowing what His sacrifice in our place would accomplish for us and for Him as well. So "for the joy that lay before him, he endured the cross, despising the shame" (Heb. 12:2). But that doesn't change the devastating reality of what He endured for us.

Withstanding His Father's withdrawal.

Not just *feeling* forsaken but *being* forsaken.

Taking our place, whatever it took.

What does the forsakenness of Jesus on the cross tell us about the nature of sin and of His sufferings?

Had Jesus not been forsaken, we would be forsaken forever. How should this affect our attitude toward sin and toward the Savior?

Lord Jesus, how can I thank You enough for being willing to be abandoned by Your Father—for my sake, that I might be forgiven and received by Him? I am unworthy of such love. I worship You.

AMEN.

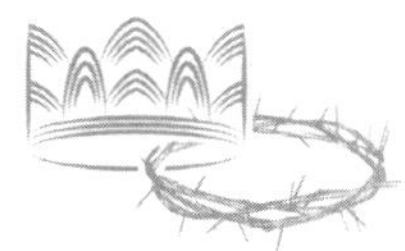

Day 35

Praying His Word

The Word of Dereliction, Part 2

My God, I cry by day, but you do not answer,
by night, yet I have no rest.
—PSALM 22:2

Throughout my decades in ministry, countless people have shared painful stories from their past with me. Among the most heartbreaking are those accounts of being wounded, abused, or abandoned by one or both parents. More often than not, these events and the resulting fall-out make it difficult for these grown children to trust in God as Father.

To comfort these friends and help them find healing and hope, I sometimes take them to Scriptures such as this one:

> Even if my father and mother abandon me,
> the LORD cares for me. (Ps. 27:10)

I've learned that God's Word—God's truth—can hold us together when we feel ourselves falling apart.

The experience of Christ on the cross illustrates this principle, showing how the Word can galvanize our faith, securing it in the bed-rock of what God has told us even when everything around us is telling us something else.

Jesus' cry of abandonment from the cross is particularly telling in this regard:

"My God, my God, why have you forsaken me?"

You see, Jesus didn't simply pull these words out of thin air or pour them from His own stream of consciousness. He already knew them well because throughout His earthly life He'd studied and meditated on them in the Old Testament Scriptures. Small wonder, then, that in His hour of greatest need He turned to His Father's Word for words to pray. And His desolation found a voice in this familiar cry from the Psalms:

> My God, my God, why have you forsaken me?
> Why are you so far from saving me, from the words of my groaning? (Ps. 22:1 ESV)

"My God, my God . . ." These ancient words of Scripture, uttered centuries later by our suffering Savior, ring out not just as a desperate cry, but also as an earnest, unshakable expression of faith. The psalmist begins his prayer by looking *up*, addressing an apparently absent God whom he trusts is still there.

Jesus, in His agony, also cried out to God. The Father's face had been eclipsed, but Jesus trusted that He was there and that He was "*my* God." Even as He cried out in grief and pain, temporarily abandoned by God, He did not doubt the reality and character of His Father. As Charles Spurgeon wrote in his commentary on the Psalms, "Oh that we could imitate this cleaving to an afflicting God!"[29]

Many commentators believe that as Jesus hung on the cross, struggling for air, steeling Himself against the pain shooting through His body, He may have recited in His mind not just the first verse, but the entirety of Psalm 22 (and perhaps the next several psalms as well). We can't be sure, of course, but the progression of this ancient Jewish hymn certainly fits what Jesus was going through.

For example, having first looked *up* to God, the psalmist then looks *around*, honestly assessing the fierce enemies that encircle him:

> I am a worm and not a man,
> scorned by mankind and despised by people.
> Everyone who sees me mocks me;

they sneer and shake their heads. . . .
Dogs have surrounded me;
a gang of evildoers has closed in on me;
they pierced my hands and my feet. (vv. 6–7, 16)

These verses (and others like them) are clearly prophetic of Jesus' experience on the cross.

But the psalmist not only looks *up* and *around*; he also looks *back*, reminding God of His mercies to saints of previous generations:

Our ancestors trusted in you;
they trusted, and you rescued them.
They cried to you and were set free;
they trusted in you and were not disgraced. (vv. 4–5)

So, too, as Jesus suffered alienation from His Father on the cross, He was surely mindful of the history of God's dealings with His people who trusted in Him to save them.

But the psalmist does not let his focus remain on the past or the present. Buoyed by God's faithfulness in the past, he looks *ahead* with assurance that God will also be faithful in the future:

All of the ends of the earth will remember
and turn to the LORD.
All the families of the nations
will bow down before you. (v. 27)

Their descendants will serve him;
the next generation will be told about the Lord.
They will come and declare his righteousness;
to a people yet to be born
they will declare what he has done. (vv. 30–31)

We know that Jesus likewise looked to the outcome of His sufferings—"the joy that lay before him" (Heb. 12:2)—as affirmed in this psalm that seems to have fueled His prayers and anchored His faith during those final hours on the cross. The psalmist's words, written centuries earlier, clearly found their ultimate fulfillment in Jesus' hour of suffering and death.

In His process of dying, Jesus would experience something that none of us, thank God, will ever go through. For the sake of our salvation, He was forsaken by His Father. But we who will *never* be forsaken or abandoned by God can draw from the same biblical well that He did. When we find ourselves in a crisis, tempted to doubt, when our emotions feel strained to the breaking point, His Word hidden in our hearts assures us that our Rock will hold, because

> He himself has said, I will never leave you or abandon you. Therefore, we may boldly say,
>
> The Lord is my helper;
> I will not be afraid.
> What can man do to me? (Heb. 13:5–6)

What practical steps could you take to have God's Word more accessible and at the front of your mind when you face trials?

When you are in distress and feeling abandoned, how can rehearsing Scripture and praying it back to God ignite faith and strengthen your heart?

Father in heaven, Your Word assures us that
You will never leave us, You will never abandon us.
It assures us that You are faithful to a thousand
generations of those who love You and call on
Your name. Help me to trust in You and in Your
promises no matter what others may do to me.
AMEN.

Day 36

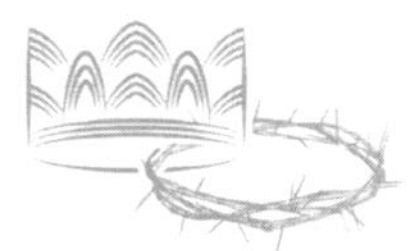

Means to an End

The Word of Agony, Part 1

This happened that the Scripture might be fulfilled.
—JOHN 19:24

"I thirst."

It's the shortest of the seven statements Jesus made from the cross. It's also among the last, one of the final four "words" apparently spoken closely together just as His life was nearing its end. Only the last few drops of the cup of suffering now remained for Him to drink.

His "word of dereliction" ("My God, my God, why have you forsaken me?") had addressed the *spiritual* aspect of His suffering—by far the most significant and severe part of His crucifixion ordeal. Earlier statements addressed His earthly relationships. Only now, as He neared the end of His six-hour battle against excruciating pain, did He say a single recorded word about the physical aspect of His suffering. But this dimension was by no means insignificant. One of the effects of crucifixion was intense dehydration, and extreme thirst was one of the worst forms of the physical distress.

How paradoxical was it that the Creator of oceans, rivers, and rain, the One who sent a flood to cover the earth, the One who caused water to gush from a rock for the children of Israel in the wilderness, now suffered from thirst. It was evidence of His humanity. God as Spirit doesn't get thirsty, but God in human flesh—Jesus—did. He fully experienced all the infirmities of our humanity apart from sin.

And just as His cry of spiritual pain was tethered to the Scripture, so now was His gasping expression of physical pain:

> Jesus, knowing that all was now finished, said (to fulfill the Scripture), "I thirst." (John 19:28 ESV)

"To fulfill the Scripture"? Yes. Numerous Old Testament prophecies had been fulfilled throughout the course of His entire life and ministry, from His birth to a virgin mother in Bethlehem to His triumphal entry into Jerusalem to the thirty pieces of silver for which Judas betrayed Him. And even here on this final day, here on the cross, events were not just happening randomly. The nailing of His feet and hands, the gambling for His clothing—it was all coming together in accordance with God's plan. Every word spoken of His earthly life in the Scripture had been fulfilled.

Everything except the one He was now experiencing:

> My strength is dried up like baked clay;
> my tongue sticks to the roof of my mouth.
> You put me into the dust of death. (Ps. 22:15)
>
> I am weary from my crying;
> my throat is parched. (Ps. 69:3)
>
> They gave me gall for my food,
> and for my thirst
> they gave me vinegar to drink. (Ps. 69:21)

To the very end, Jesus' life (and death) was marked by His deep respect and reverence for the Word of God. He took great care not only to obey it but also to fulfill it. So as His death drew near, He stirred the remaining embers of His strength. Heaving His body upward, pushing down against the violently inflamed tissue in His torn feet and ankles, He summoned just enough breath to make His voice audible. And He spoke the words "I thirst," thus fulfilling this remaining Messianic prophecy.

This leaves me to wonder: do you and I care that much about the Scripture? Do we love God's Word that deeply? When we're suffering physically—or in *any* way, really—do we remain focused on reflecting Him well? Do we honor His Word in our responses?

To the very end, Jesus' life (and death) was marked by His deep respect and reverence for the Word of God. Do you and I care that much about the Scripture?

First Peter 5:7, for example, says to cast "all your cares on him, because he cares about you." When we're under pressure, when we're dealing with more than we think we can handle, do we demonstrate to those around us what it looks like to trust God with our cares? Do we give them an opportunity to see how beautifully He cares for our troubles?

And then there's the matter of gratitude. First Thessalonians 5:18 exhorts us to "give thanks in everything." When we're feeling outnumbered by hardships, when we think we're being treated and talked about unfairly, are we intent on fulfilling this Scripture? Do we exhibit the uncommon gratitude God's Word says is possible for His children?

I confess: Whenever I'm the one talking about being thirsty or hungry or tired, I'm prone to say it with a whine. I'm thinking mostly about myself and how I feel, about how my life at that moment is not giving me what I want. I'm not saying it the way Jesus said it, with an eye toward manifesting to others the trustworthiness of God's Word.

"I thirst."

He said the words, and up came a sponge dipped in the "sour wine" (John 19:29) that was sitting there for the soldiers to drink. Someone soaked a sponge in the vinegary swill, jabbed the filthy wad onto the sharp end of a hyssop branch, and held it up to Jesus' mouth. Who knows why the person felt impressed to do it? It was the only thing resembling kindness anyone had done for Him during this six-hour odyssey. Little did that individual know he was involved in fulfilling a thousand-year-old prophecy from the Word of almighty God.

But Jesus knew. That's why Jesus said it. And as we become more and more like Him, we'll desire that the Word of God be fulfilled in us and through us.

At all times. For His glory.

What current circumstances are bringing you difficulty? How might you react differently to these if your desire was to prove God's Word true in the midst of it?

How have you seen others live out the heart of Scripture when they are in distress, and how has this affected you?

Lord, thank You for giving me Your Word—to speak to me, guide me, instruct me, and inspire me. May I never dismiss or discount its message, thinking it's impractical, not applicable, or impossible to implement. Rather, help me see each circumstance You allow into my life as an opportunity for me to communicate Your truth to those around me. As Jesus did.

AMEN.

Day 37

Dying Thirst, Living Water

The Word of Agony, Part 2

"If anyone is thirsty, let him come to me and drink."
—JOHN 7:37

Jesus had been parched for a long time before His cry of agonizing thirst near the end of His ordeal. Within a period of twenty-four hours—through the events in Gethsemane, His trial, and His crucifixion—He had lost a lot of bodily fluids, both sweat and blood. And yet He'd also turned down at least one attempt to ease His discomfort.

You may recall that moment earlier in the day, when the soldiers charged with the execution "tried to give him wine mixed with myrrh" (Mark 15:23)—or "mixed with gall," as another gospel says (Matt. 27:34). But as thirsty as He was, Jesus had refused to drink the concoction.

Why?

The blended contents of this drink were intended to function as a sedative, to take the edge off the crippling pain every crucifixion victim experienced. It was offered to prisoners, I suspect, mainly to stop their irritating screaming. But regardless of the motivation, it still offered a measure of relief.

If I were in Jesus' place, enduring such intense physical agony, I suspect I'd accept whatever anyone offered to alleviate the dizzying discomfort. Wouldn't you? But Jesus wasn't interested in easing His suffering, only in accomplishing His mission: to love and obey the Father and to sacrifice His life for us. So He'd declined the pain-numbing potion. He wanted to be in full possession of His senses (to experience the full cup of suffering and fully pay the price for our sin) and to keep His mind clear (to meditate on Scripture and to pray).

Only now, with His sufferings near an end and the cup of God's wrath nearly drained, did He cry out about His thirst. Only now did He accept a measure of relief, a sponge dipped in sour wine—likely cheap wine used by common people and soldiers, highly diluted with water—effectively moistening His parched lips and enabling Him to make a final triumphant shout before He died.

Actually, it's an amazing demonstration of self-control that only once during those six excruciating hours on the cross did He cry out regarding His physical suffering. He'd had no food, no water, no pain-killers, no relief for His human appetites and needs—all while being cut off from fellowship with the Father. And He did it for us, who tend to be so preoccupied with getting our needs met and our cravings fulfilled that we find it difficult to deny ourselves for even a brief time.

Jesus' physical thirst, of course, reflected the thirst His soul experienced. In His plea from the cross, we can almost hear the plaintive cry of Psalm 42:

> As a deer longs for flowing streams,
> so I long for you, God.
> I thirst for God, the living God.
> When can I come and appear before God? (vv. 1–2)

He'd been walking this earth for thirty-three years now. He'd endured the censure and contempt that accompanied His divine calling. He'd done it perfectly, painfully, and finally He was within inches and minutes of the finish line. So He was longing for home. Longing for God.

Suffering here in human flesh, forsaken by God, Jesus was dying to be restored into fellowship with His Father. No earthly taste or tranquilizer could offer Him what only the treasures of heaven could provide. And if you and I ever expect to feel that kind of satisfaction inside, we must get this same reality through our minds as well. Nothing—*nothing*—satisfies as He satisfies. So Jesus the man was thirsting for God.

As Jesus suffered, He endured the torments of hell, one of which is unquenchable thirst. I am struck by the contrast between Jesus' admission of thirst from the cross and that of another man in Scripture who complained of thirst from beyond the grave. Jesus once told the story of a rich man who feasted "lavishly every day" (Luke 16:19) but died an unbelieving death and found himself "in torment in Hades" (v. 23). Trapped there in eternal anguish, he cried out across the divide: "Have mercy on me and send Lazarus [the "poor man" in the parable] to dip the tip of his finger in water and cool my tongue, because I am in agony in this flame!" (v. 24).

Jesus endured intense physical thirst on the cross so our spiritual thirst might be relieved and satisfied. He's given us "living water" to drink—one of the gifts of the gospel, granted to thirsty, believing hearts.

That's where you and I would be—dying of thirst for all eternity—if Jesus had not endured these hours of separation from God on our behalf. His cry of thirst reflected the anguish of His soul as He tasted the fires of God's judgment for all mankind. He was thirsting on our behalf.

Jesus endured intense physical thirst on the cross so our spiritual thirst might be relieved and satisfied. He's given us "living water" to drink—one of the gifts of the gospel, granted to thirsty, believing hearts.

> "If anyone is thirsty, let him come to me and drink. The one who believes in me, as the Scripture has said, will have streams of living water flow from deep within him." (John 7:37–38)

The thirst in our hearts will never be quenched through anyone or anything other than Jesus. So "let the one who is thirsty come" (Rev. 22:17) because Jesus has already thirsted for our sake. "Let the one who desires take the water of life freely" (v. 17), for Jesus is the water of life who fully, deeply, and eternally satisfies our longing souls.

In what ways have you found the relief and resources of this world to be unsatisfying and insufficient to quench the thirst of your soul?

How have you experienced Jesus' ability to satisfy the longings of your heart with His "living water"?

I give You thanks, Lord Jesus, for all You endured on our behalf. I am not worthy. I should have been the one thirsting on the cross. But You endured thirst in Your body as well as separation from Your Father and the unquenchable torment of hell—so that I could be filled with living water. Praise You, Lord, for this unspeakable gift. I thirst only for You.

AMEN.

Day 38

Nailing the Finish

The Word of Triumph, Part 1

"I have glorified You on the earth. I have finished the work which You have given Me to do."

—JOHN 17:4 NKJV

The story is told of a nineteenth-century business magnate and politician who cried out on his deathbed, "So little done, so much to do!"[30]

How strikingly different was the sentiment expressed by our Savior in prayer as He approached His time to die, affirming that He had completed the work His Father had given Him to do on the earth (John 17:4).

If I could say that at the end of my earthly life, I could surely close my eyes in peace.

No matter how long I have left on earth, it won't be enough to complete everything *I* want to get done—all the plans, dreams, and projects that have filled my to-do lists for as long as I can remember. And I surely will never be able to finish all the things *other people* have said or thought I should do. You can probably relate. But wouldn't you like to say with me—wouldn't we all love to say with the Lord Jesus—that we completed all the work *our Father* gave us to do during our time on this earth?

There's a word for that feeling: *tetelestai!*

And Jesus, in the waning moments of His life, was able to roar it in triumph.

Tetelestai! That Greek verb as it appears in the gospel of John (19:30) may truly be the single greatest word ever spoken in the history of humankind. Most of our English-language Bibles translate it with three words:

"It is finished."

Some even punctuate it with an exclamation point—and appropriately so. The parallel accounts of Matthew and Mark, although neither of them includes this exact word, describe Jesus crying out "with a loud voice" (Matt. 27:50), uttering "a loud cry" (Mark 15:37).

It is finished! Of all tasks ever undertaken in all the centuries of human civilization, none was more impossible to achieve, yet more perfectly accomplished, than the life Jesus lived. He came to earth on a mission, and He fulfilled it exactly as planned.

Now, depending on how it is read and interpreted, this English translation could be understood in entirely different ways:

- "It is finished" could sound like *relief*—"Whew! Finally!"—said with a huge sigh. "Am I ever glad that's over!"
- "It is finished" could sound like *despair,* said with more of a whimper, giving the impression of His being completely undone by this whole affair.
- "It is finished" could sound like *defeat,* spoken as a concession to failure, as if He'd tried and done His best, but in the end, well, it had just gotten the best of Him.

But is that what we're supposed to hear in His voice? Relief? Despair? Defeat?

Not at all!

Tetelestai is a form of the Greek verb *teleō,* which means "to bring to an end, to complete, to accomplish."[31] It signifies "to finish . . . to carry out a thing to the full."[32]

Try placing yourself in that moment before Jesus takes His final breath on the cross. The sky is black in the middle of the day. Perhaps the wind is picking up. There's a charged intensity in the air. Suddenly the "loud voice" of Jesus crackles above the mumbling din of the soldiers milling about, above the muffled sobs of the few people within earshot who are mourning His cruel, undeserved treatment.

"It is finished."

Finished! It's a cry of jubilation! The shout of a victor! F. W. Krummacher captured its power in his wonderful book, *The Suffering Saviour*:

> These are the greatest and most momentous words that were ever spoken upon earth, since the beginning of the world. . . . It is a shout of triumph, which announces to the kingdom of darkness its complete overthrow and to the kingdom of heaven upon earth its eternal establishment. . . . Listen, and it will appear to you as if in the words, "It is finished!" you heard fetters burst, and prison-walls fall down. At these words, barriers as high as heaven are overthrown, and gates which had been closed for thousands of years, again move on their hinges.[33]

We do not have to accomplish everything we may feel pressed to do during our short span on this planet. Our task is to complete what *our Father* gives us to do.

Jesus had always taken seriously the purpose for which He had been sent to earth. We hear it in His first recorded words when He was in the temple at age twelve, speaking to His concerned parents: "Did you not know that I must be about My Father's business?" (Luke 2:49 NKJV).

He had focused on that business throughout His earthly life. And now, some twenty years after that temple visit,

Jesus attested that He had completed every assignment God had given Him. He had healed every person He was to heal, delivered every message He was to deliver, fulfilled every prophecy regarding His earthly ministry. Most important, He had offered up His life as a sacrifice for sinners.

Tetelestai is a word a first-century servant might have used when he'd completed the task assigned to him by his employer. Now Jesus used it to report that His life's work on earth was finished. In His cry of "It is finished," we can hear the exhilaration of a mission accomplished. He had not carried out every task that others might have wished of Him. But He had succeeded in the entire purpose for which His Father had sent Him to earth.

What does that mean for us? For starters, it means that we do not have to accomplish everything we may feel pressed to do during our short span on this planet. Our task is to complete what *He* gives us to do. And our risen Savior lives within us to make it possible for us to know, when we come to the end of our earthly journey, that we have glorified Him by doing just that.

In what ways do you tend to measure success in life by your own or another person's standards?

How might focusing on completing the work God has given you to do affect your thinking, decisions, and daily life?

Father, how grateful I am for the faithfulness and obedience to Your calling that Jesus demonstrated throughout His entire life. Help me discern and carry out Your assignments for whatever time You've placed me here on this earth. May You be glorified through my life.

AMEN.

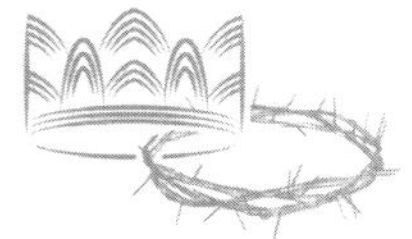

Day 39

A Complete Performance

The Word of Triumph, Part 2

There is therefore now no condemnation
for those who are in Christ Jesus.
—ROMANS 8:1 ESV

"It is finished" (*tetelestai*) is in fact a world of words. The great nineteenth-century preacher Charles Spurgeon, without overstating the point in the slightest, said, "It would need all the words that ever were spoken, or ever can be spoken, to explain this one word."[34]

To get a fuller understanding of the richness of *tetelestai,* the many facets of "It is finished," let's take a moment to consider *what* was finished. In yesterday's reading we saw that Jesus had finished the work God sent Him to do on the earth, much as a servant or employee might report to his master upon completing an assignment: "It is finished!"

Yet despite the significance of this lifetime achievement, this still doesn't explain the entirety or the enormity of *tetelestai.* Here are several examples of what His finished work encompassed and what it means for us:

1. "It is finished!" meant Jesus' suffering was over. This assures us that our earthly suffering will one day end as well.

From the moment He left heaven's glory to come to this earth, Jesus was no stranger to suffering. The Creator of the world became a needy infant born in a cattle shed. As a toddler He was hunted by Herod, forced to flee to Egypt with His parents. As an adult He often experienced exhaustion, loneliness, physical want, and personal threats. He was confronted, ridiculed, and marginalized by His enemies, betrayed and forsaken by His friends. Finally, on the cross, He drained the entire cup of suffering until not one drop remained. He had finished it all.

What a comfort this should be to us. One day, because of the suffering He endured for our sakes, we'll be able say "It is finished" to our suffering too. No more tears, no more pain, no more sickness, no more broken relationships, no more death. The soreness, sadness, and anxieties of this life, though serious and upsetting in the present, will be less than a dim memory. In assigning an expiration date to all suffering, Jesus has guaranteed us a joyful, pain-free eternity.

2. "It is finished!" meant the price of sin had been paid in full. As a result, there is no more payment required for our sin.

"The wages of sin is death" (Rom. 6:23). That is the price we deserved to pay. But the good news of the gospel is that Jesus paid it all! God was fully satisfied by the price of Jesus' blood. For us to try to add something of our own effort to this work would be akin to having a generous friend pay off our mortgage but then return to the bank month after month trying to make another payment! No, your sin debt has been paid in full. It is finished.

3. "It is finished!" meant the eternal plan of redemption was now complete. There is nothing further for us to do in order to be rescued from God's wrath.

God is not waiting on us to do anything more to earn our place at His table. Jesus has already claimed that for us. In Him the work of salvation has been accomplished. Every demand of God's righteous law has been fulfilled. The storm of God's wrath toward us is expended, His justice fully satisfied. The doorway to paradise stands open with no obstacles or barriers to prevent us from enjoying full fellowship with

Him as His sons and daughters. Because "it is finished," our redemption is a done deal. All we can do is humbly receive it in repentance and faith.

4. "It is finished!" meant the old covenant was finished. Therefore, we no longer need to carry out those burdensome regulations and rituals.

Old Testament worshipers were all too familiar with endless ordinances required to deal with their sin and guilt—going before the priest, ceremonial washings, killing animals, shedding blood, offering sacrifices. Again and again and again. But as the author of Hebrews explained, these rituals were "symbolic of the present time" (Heb. 9:9), intended to point toward the work of Christ on the cross. Our incomparable Jesus—the Lamb of God, the acceptable Sacrifice, our great High Priest—replaced those symbols and shadows with the reality of redemption. So we have no more need of endless, elaborate rituals to take care of our sin.

One day, because of the suffering He endured for our sakes, we'll be able to say "It is finished" to our suffering too. The soreness, sadness, and anxieties of this life will be less than a dim memory.

5. "It is finished" meant the battle against Satan and sin had been won. Our fiercest enemy is now a defeated foe.

Imagine the victory Satan thought he'd won when he saw Jesus nailed to the cross. How he must have gloated: *"'It is finished'? Ha! Finished indeed."* But Satan got it all wrong—because he was the one who was finished.

Yes, the devil still lurks, "prowling around like a roaring lion, looking for anyone he can devour" (1 Peter 5:8). But Christ took on human flesh "so that through his death he might destroy the one holding the power of death—that is, the devil—and free those who were held in slavery all their lives by the fear of death" (Heb. 2:14–15). The one who had the power of death was defeated by the One who stripped him of his power by dying. And the enemy lost his advantage over us forever.

The end of suffering. The full payment for our sin debt. The culmination of God's redemptive plan. The end of the old covenant symbols. Victory over Satan. *Tetelestai* means these things and so much more. In the words of the classic Easter hymn,

> Love's redeeming work is done, Alleluia!
> Fought the fight, the battle won, Alleluia![35]

"It is finished," indeed. Alleluia! Amen.

Is there an area of your life where you sometimes find yourself trying to do something Jesus has already finished for you? By faith, thank God for the finished work of Christ in that area.

When are you most susceptible to doubting you're accepted by God? How would you encourage another believer who felt that way?

Thank You, Father, that in Christ everything has been completed to ensure that we could have an eternal, right standing with You. Help me to receive Your provision and not to forfeit my peace by giving way to doubt or fear or trying to accomplish the work Jesus has already finished.

AMEN.

Day 40

Into His Hands

The Word of Confidence, Part 1

Then Jesus, calling out with a loud voice, said, "Father, into your hands I commit my spirit!"

—LUKE 23:46 ESV

Return with me to Gethsemane—less than twenty-four hours before Jesus' final moments on the cross.

Jesus is praying. His disciples sleep. Beads of blood form on His brow even as the footsteps of Judas draw closer, surrounded by a detachment of temple police. With a determined sigh Jesus rouses His drowsy disciples: "Are you still sleeping and resting? See, the time is near. The Son of Man is betrayed into the hands of sinners" (Matt. 26:45).

And, oh, what the hands of those sinners will do to Him.

Flail and torture Him.

Craft crude symbols of royalty and use them for mockery.

Drive nails through His bare flesh.

Stage His baseless, public execution.

And though Jesus could easily summon "more than twelve legions of angels" (Matt. 26:53) to disarm His opponents, He voluntarily submits Himself to those people.

To those plans.

To those hands.

I recently asked a friend about some scars visible on her arms and legs. Her response left me deeply saddened and shaken. The marks told the tale of wounds inflicted by the hands of one abuser after another, over the course of years. "One man used my back as a human ash tray," she confided.

Though the details may differ, no doubt you, too, have suffered losses and injustices at the hands of others. We all have. Those people and their perverse plans have caused us significant pain. And our reflexive response is to focus our anger and resentment on those who have wounded us, to build a case for how they've ruined the trajectories of our lives, bringing harm and misery to us, stealing opportunities that could've been ours if not for what they did to us. Out of such selfish motives and actions.

But Jesus knew, and we can know, that our lives belong to no one but God. Now and forever, they rest in the Father's safe, secure, and protective hands.

And so Jesus in His final moments, after crying "My God, my God" with such agonizing passion, shifted His heavenward focus once more. No longer appealing to "God," as if from a distance, He now addressed His "Father," whose smile and presence were once again palpably real to Him:

"Father, into your hands I commit my spirit."

The raw weather conditions that since noon had shrouded the cross in darkness continued unabated. The agony of the cross—the scorching pain from lacerated sinews in His wrists and feet, the strain on his lungs from trying to breathe while hanging there—was no less acute, no more bearable. But with His remaining breaths reduced now to single digits, Jesus knew His ordeal was coming to an end.

"The time is near," He'd said to His disciples in Gethsemane when Judas approached Him in the garden with treachery in his heart and his greeting.

Now on Golgotha's hill, the time was finally, mercifully here. The time for those same hands of God that had wounded His Son on the cross to widen into a welcoming embrace.

Those hands—they held Him.

God's hands—they hold us.

Now flash back with me again to a brighter moment on the kingdom calendar, to a sunny day before Jesus felt the whip and the thorns—a beautiful red-letter page in our Bibles that tells of a good Shepherd who has come to give us abundant life.

Jesus is in Jerusalem, walking freely in the temple not far from the place where His cross will eventually be erected. Members of the Jewish leadership class approach and ask Him sarcastically if He's the Messiah: "Don't keep us in suspense."

Jesus doesn't take the bait. "I did tell you," He replies, referencing "the works that I do in my Father's name." Then He added, "You don't believe because you are not of my sheep" (John 10:26). But those who *do* believe, those who *are* His sheep (as *we* are) can rest in the following promise: "My sheep hear my voice, I know them, and they follow me. I give them eternal life, and they will never perish. *No one will snatch them out of my hand*" (vv. 27–28).

Jesus knew, and we can know, that our lives belong to no one but God. Now and forever, they rest in the Father's safe, secure, and protective hands.

Out of *Jesus'* hand. The *Son's* hand.

We are eternally safe in His hands. He is forever in the Father's hands:

"Father, into your hands I commit my spirit."

And because the Son is with the Father, we are safe in the Father's hands as well. As Jesus went on to say during that John 10 day, "My Father, who has given them to me, is greater than all. No one is able to snatch them out of the Father's hand" (v. 29).

Think about it: Our lives are in the hands of the Son, which means they are in the hands of the Father. The hands into which Jesus committed Himself after others had done their worst to Him.

So let's not listen any longer to the voices insisting that our lives have been wrecked by the interfering, cruel hands of others.

Lift your eyes, as He lifted His weary eyes, above the people and circumstances that have caused such real and lasting pain. And commit yourself by faith into your Father's hands, where you are assured of always being received with love and handled with care.

Your Father's hands, which hold you and will never let you go.

Given your own set of circumstances, what would committing yourself to the Father's hands look like and mean?

What situations or parts of your life do you struggle to commit to His care? By faith, thank Him now that your life is in His hands and that He can be trusted to carry and to care for you all the way to heaven.

Father, thank You that my life is not in the hands of fate or chance, of circumstances or difficult people, but in Your loving and capable hands. There is no safer place I could be. Thank You for being utterly trustworthy, fully powerful, and eternally faithful. Make me a testimony of Your grace and glory.

AMEN.

Day 41 | *Good Friday*

A Matter of Death and Life

The Word of Confidence, Part 2

Bowing his head, he gave up his spirit.

—JOHN 19:30

Jesus died as He had lived: praying, forgiving, loving, sacrificing, meditating on Scripture, and entrusting Himself to His Father. Which raises this question for each of us: If I die as I have lived, how will I die? If you and I hope to have these resources at our disposal when we come to the end of our earthly lives, we must become acquainted with them now.

Our Savior had suffered in total darkness for three long hours. He had endured an eternity of suffering in that span. Now it was time (God's time) for Him to breathe His last.

Jesus had assured His disciples that "no one" could take His life from Him, that He laid it down of His own volition (John 10:18). And His essence didn't just ebb away, flickering out after a futile fight for survival. Most victims of crucifixion lingered on much longer than He did, sometimes writhing for days before death finally overpowered them. But Jesus wasn't conquered by death. Instead, by His death He conquered death.

That doesn't mean we won't die, of course. "The dust returns to the earth as it once was" (Eccl. 12:7), and we can do nothing to stop it from happening. Yet, thanks to Jesus, death need not be the end for us.

This is the reality expressed by Jesus in His seventh and final word from the cross:

> Jesus, calling out with a loud voice, said, *"Father, into your hands I commit my spirit!"* (Luke 23:46 ESV)

Jesus handed over His soul to the keeping of His Father, to whom He would return shortly.

F. B. Meyer explains this beautifully in his book *Love to the Uttermost,* suggesting that Jesus' next-to-last statement—"It is finished"—served as His "farewell to the world He was leaving," but that His final word—"Father, into your hands I commit my spirit"—served as His "greeting" to the world He was about to enter.

> It seems as though the Spirit of Christ was poising itself before it departed to the Father, and it saw before [it] no dismal abyss, no gulf of darkness, no footless chaos, but hands, even the hands of the Father—and to these He committed Himself.[36]

This picture of Christ poised at the threshold, looking ahead in trust and love, moves me deeply when I think about my own inevitable death. He exhibited no paralyzing fear at the prospect of leaving this earth. Nor does the prospect of dying need to terrify those of us who are in Him.

To be sure, we are not promised our deaths will be easy. Jesus' body was mangled, ravaged with pain on the cross. Our final hours, too, may be marked by pain or trauma. Yet His dying words assure us our spirits will follow Him safely into God's presence, where we will live with Him and with our Father forever. He died with resurrection—both His and ours—already in His eyes.

We have seen that Jesus had Scripture in His heart while suffering on the cross, as He cried out those anguished words from Psalm 22: "My God . . . why have you forsaken me?" Now in these final moments of His earthly life He uttered a prayer from another psalm that was on His mind: "Into your hand I commit my spirit" (Ps. 31:5). And then, Luke's gospel tells us, He "breathed His last" (23:46).

Matthew's gospel makes clear that Jesus did not die as a helpless victim or even a passive martyr. Rather, we are told, "He yielded up his spirit" (27:50 ESV). He died as a voluntary act of His will, in obedience to the Father. He placed His life on the altar—willingly, consciously giving it up as a sacrifice. Despite the violent, torturous mistreatment He'd endured, Jesus died with peace and confidence, knowing His life was secure in the Father's hands.

Jesus' dying words assure us our spirits will follow Him safely into God's presence, where we will live with Him and with our Father forever. He died with resurrection—both His and ours—already in His eyes.

And the same confidence can be ours as we draw near to death's door.

That's not true for everyone, of course. Those who have not believed in Christ and committed their lives into God's hand for safekeeping will one day be turned over to His hand for judgment. And Scripture warns that "it is a terrifying thing to fall into the hands of the living God" (Heb. 10:31).

But for us who have trusted Christ for salvation, who have committed our souls into His hands, the fear of death can be overcome by the anticipation of spending eternity in His presence.

With that in mind, take a look at the words from Psalm 31 that formed Jesus' final prayer before being ushered into the Father's embrace:

> In you, O LORD, do I take refuge;
> let me never be put to shame;
> in your righteousness deliver me! . . .
> Into your hand I commit my spirit;
> you have redeemed me, O LORD, faithful God. (Ps. 31:1, 5 ESV)

You and I, too, can make these words our prayer, trusting that as we commit our lives into the Father's hand, He will take us all the way through death into eternal life.

How can the way Jesus died calm our natural fears and doubts about facing our own death?

The apostle Paul affirmed, "I know whom I have believed and am persuaded that he is able to guard what has been entrusted to me until that day" (2 Tim. 1:12). How can this perspective give you confidence as you contemplate the end of your life here on earth?

Thank You, Lord, for the peace and assurance that result from knowing my life and my times—including my death—are in Your keeping. Help me commit myself and all my concerns—past, present, and future—into Your wise, loving, and gracious care.

AMEN.

Part Four

NOW AND FOREVER WITH CHRIST

Love's redeeming work is done;
fought the fight, the battle won:
lo, our Sun's eclipse is o'er,
lo, he sets in blood no more.

Vain the stone, the watch, the seal;
Christ has burst the gates of hell;
death in vain forbids him rise;
Christ has opened paradise. . . .

Soar we now where Christ has led,
following our exalted Head;
made like him, like him we rise;
ours the cross, the grave, the skies.

—Charles Wesley[37]

Day 42

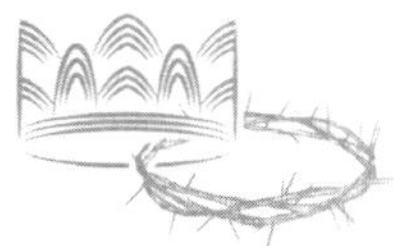

Behind the Curtain

The Calvary Miracles, Part 1

Then the curtain of the temple was torn in two from top to bottom.
—MARK 15:38

The cross is our defining moment—history's watershed event. It's where everything that ever mattered was always leading, where everything that matters today is still measured. And to prove to us that Christ's death on the cross was this kind of happening—an event like none other—God made sure its effect was not confined to one isolated hill outside Jerusalem.

He did this by surrounding the moment with miracles.

These were not the first miracles associated with Jesus' life, of course. The four Gospels together report on more than three dozen He had already performed before this moment. These supernatural works had not only transformed the lives of people He encountered but had also served as signs that He was indeed the Messiah, declaring the kingdom of heaven to all who would receive it. So it certainly made kingdom sense for additional miracles to attend the triumph of Jesus' crucifixion and resurrection.

These "Calvary miracles" included the mysterious daytime darkness that preceded Jesus' death (Matt. 27:45) and the sudden jarring of an earthquake that immediately followed (vv. 51, 54), resulting in the opening of rock tombs and the appearance of saints who had previously died. (We'll take a closer look at this miracle in a couple of days.)

Remarkable as all this was, the most symbolically spectacular miracle happened in the temple. At the precise moment when Jesus "gave up his spirit" (v. 50), the immense, intricately embroidered curtain separating the "holy place" from the "most holy place" (often called the "holy of holies") was split in half, torn down the middle "from top to bottom."

A quick explanation of what all this meant. Behind this grand curtain sat the ark of the covenant, topped by the "mercy seat" where God had met with His people (Ex. 25:22) from ancient times. But by Old Testament ceremonial law, this holy of holies could only be entered once a year, on the Day of Atonement. And then, only by the high priest, who would offer a sacrifice of blood for the sins of the people as well as for his own sins, since not even this appointed representative was above needing his sins forgiven.

This curtain, then, was an ornate, elaborate "Keep Out" sign, separating the presence and glory of almighty God from His sinful people. No access allowed—not without blood, and even then only rarely.

But Jesus' death changed everything.

He died at three in the afternoon. To the Jews who had assembled in Jerusalem for Passover week, it was the hour of the evening sacrifice. So imagine you were one of the priests officiating in the temple that day—serving outside the curtain, of course, assisting the gathered worshipers who had lined up to present their offerings.

The altar was aglow with fire. The blood of sacrifice was flowing freely. Then, suddenly, came a loud tearing sound. *The curtain!*

This curtain wasn't just a thin piece of fabric one might use as a window covering. The original instructions for its creation, dating back to the days of Solomon's temple, called for it to be made of blue, purple, and crimson yarn with the imagery of angelic cherubim woven into it (2 Chron. 3:14). It was thirty feet wide and sixty feet high. Drawing from sources of the temple era, nineteenth-century historian and Bible scholar Alfred Edersheim tells us that the veil was "the thickness of the palm of a hand" and so heavy that it required three hundred priests to handle it.[38]

Yet at the hour of Christ's death, this massive textile ripped in half like a sheet of paper and crumpled to the ground in a massive heap, scissored by an unseen hand. And suddenly a sacred space that was functionally off limits to everyone, which only one person was given the privilege of entering once each year, lay fully unveiled.

Picture the shock: the stunned expressions, the mouths hanging open, the inability of those in the temple to turn their gaze away, paired with the natural reflex to shield their eyes from seeing too much. Who could bear to stand exposed, unprotected, before the holy presence of God?

Answer: *anybody* . . . now that God had received the death of His Son, the death of the Lamb, as the final sacrifice for sin.

The rending of the temple curtain dramatically signified the end of the old covenant system. Jesus had "entered the most holy place once for all time, not by the blood of goats and calves, but by his own blood, having obtained eternal redemption" (Heb. 9:12). The infinite chasm that existed between God and humanity had been bridged. The curtain that once said "Keep Out" now proclaimed, by its notable absence, "Come In." Come *boldly*. Draw near. You are welcome here, welcome in the very presence of God.

The curtain that once said "Keep Out" now proclaimed, by its notable absence, "Come In." Come *boldly*. Draw near. You are welcome here, welcome in the very presence of God.

That invitation is still there for you, for me, for all who believe. And it's still nothing short of miraculous.

Christ's flesh had been torn at Calvary. His spirit had been torn from His flesh at the moment of His death. And the cosmic reverberations of all this tearing had made their way through the ground, into the city, into the temple, and right into the holy of holies, ripping up whatever could prevent us from meeting with God at that mercy seat.

The misery of the crucifixion had become the miracle of anytime access.

And we still can't tear ourselves away.

What if free and open access to God's presence was as shockingly new to us today as it seemed to those first observers? How would we treat it differently?

Whenever God seems quiet and distant, what can your understanding of the torn curtain do to strengthen and solidify your faith?

Heavenly Father, what a mercy it is to be welcomed into Your holy presence. I can't imagine being left to stand outside with no way to speak with You or hear from You or draw near to You. Thank You, Lord Jesus, for offering Yourself as a sacrifice in our place so that the barrier between us and the Father might be torn down. Because of You, we can boldly approach Him and never again be separated from Him.

AMEN.

Day 43 | *Resurrection Sunday*

Easter Every Day

The Resurrection of Christ

"He is not here. For he has risen, just as he said."
—MATTHEW 28:6

Happy Resurrection Day! If you've been working through this book in conjunction with the Lenten season, then today should actually be Easter Sunday. But even if you've been following a different plan (or no plan at all), this joyous sentiment is still appropriate. Because for those of us who follow Christ, every day is in a sense a celebration of this magnificent, miraculous event.

As we've seen, the cross of Christ is central to the gospel story. It was the supreme act of sacrificial love in the history of mankind. But Jesus' resurrection completes that story in triumph. It turned despair and apparent defeat into eternal hope and victory. Together these two events form the hinge of human history. They are what makes Jesus truly incomparable—and what sets the Christian faith apart from all other religions.

While no one ever lived quite as Jesus did, other people *have* lived.

And while no one ever died quite as Jesus did, other people *have* died.

But no one—no one!—has ever been raised from the dead, never to die again, as Jesus was.

So the resurrection makes all the difference. As you read the New Testament, you realize that it matters supremely. Apart from Jesus' resurrection, you and I have no hope of eternal life (see 1 Peter 1:3). The cross without the empty tomb is simply not enough. But Jesus, our unparalleled Jesus, is always enough.

So on this momentous day, let's spend a few more moments together than usual, to meditate on seven implications of the resurrection. What difference does the empty tomb make for those who have placed their faith in Christ—not just today, but next week and the next? What difference does it make when we are facing pain or tears or failure or fears?

1. The resurrection means there is hope in the most desperate circumstance.

It means God is all-powerful and can make a way out where there appears to be no way out. It means that one day all tears will be wiped away and all sorrow will be turned to joy.

Easter reminds us that God has defeated death by walking through it and that no matter how many enemies seek to take Him down, He can never die again. So when we walk through natural or relational disasters, the collapse of our health or of the economy, we can take a deep breath and know that He is alive and seated on His throne, in charge, no matter how dark it gets.

No situation, no matter how desperate, is beyond God's ability to control its outcome. The God who on that day turned death into life is the One who *every* day "makes the dawn out of darkness" (Amos 4:13).

So no matter what your day holds, hope is not dead.

In Christ, hope is always alive.

2. The resurrection means God always keeps His promises.

The resurrection was only a surprise because people didn't believe what they were told. How many prophecies had spelled out what would happen when the Messiah came? And how many times had Jesus alerted His disciples to the fact that He would "suffer" and "be rejected" and "be killed"—*and "be raised"* (Luke 9:22)? He said it again and again, but they just didn't hear and believe it. And the result was unnecessary stress, anxiety, and fear.

How different would our lives be if we really laid hold of the promises of God, if we believed He means what He says? The resurrection is the resounding *amen* to every promise God has made.

3. The resurrection means death is no longer to be feared.

No one looks forward to dying. And no one is happy when death separates us from those we love. But as Jesus compassionately assured a grieving friend, "I am the resurrection and the life. The one who believes in me, even if he dies, will live" (John 11:25–26). So although death on this earth is inevitable—and painful—it need not terrify us, because the resurrection reminds us that death is not the end, that our separations and losses are temporary.

You or someone you love may be facing a terminal illness. Ask yourself: If Jesus is the Resurrection and the Life, what do I have to fear? What is the worst that can happen? Is it death? Jesus' resurrection assures us that death has been put to death!

4. The resurrection assures us of our own bodily resurrection.

Nineteenth-century pastor Phillips Brooks once wrote, "Let [us] say not merely, 'Christ has risen,' but '*I shall rise.*'"[39] You and I are active participants in the resurrection story. The apostle Paul wrote, "God raised up the Lord and will also raise us up by his power" (1 Cor. 6:14). Christ's physical resurrection is a pledge of our own future resurrection, when God "will transform our lowly body to be like his glorious body" (Phil. 3:21 ESV).

5. The resurrection means God, in accepting Christ's work, accepts us as well.

"It is finished," remember? The resurrection was proof that God had accepted the payment Christ made for sin on the cross, that His righteous anger against sinners had been completely satisfied, and that He fully approved of Christ's death. Since we have been united with

Christ in His death (Rom. 6:3) and since God has "raised us up with him and seated us with him in the heavens" (Eph. 2:6), we are assured that we are now wholly acceptable to Him. Our guilt has been completely removed, Jesus' righteousness has been credited to our account, and God accepts and approves of us as He approves of Christ.

The cross of Christ is central to the gospel story. It was the supreme act of sacrificial love in the history of mankind. But Jesus' resurrection completes that story in triumph.

6. The resurrection means the power of sin has been overcome.

Do you struggle to break free from sinful habits and patterns? Life as fallen people means we're still capable of sinning. But life lived by faith in the resurrected Christ means we don't *have* to sin. As Romans 6 puts it, "Just as Christ was raised from the dead by the glory of the Father, so we too may walk in newness of life" (v. 4). We who have been united with Jesus in His death have also been united with Him "in the likeness of his resurrection" (v. 5). This means we are to "consider [ourselves] dead to sin and alive to God in Christ Jesus" (v. 11). It means that we no longer have to give in to sin, that we can say no to sinful desires (see v. 12).

In other words, sin doesn't rule us anymore. The resurrection changed all those rules.

7. The resurrection means resurrection power is available to us.

Don't do Easter the same old way this year. In fact, don't do this *year* the same old way. Don't just reflect back to one day long ago that still shows up on the calendar every spring. Jesus walked out of that grave to change how we do *every* day. The same power God used to raise Him from the dead is available to us (Eph. 1:18–21)—power to obey, to defeat temptation, to love and forgive, and to face every challenge with grace, assurance, and peace.

Power to live this resurrection life—so that every day is Easter Day.

How could keeping Christ's resurrection in mind each day change the way you think about all of life?

Is there any challenge you face that is greater than His resurrection power? What would walking in the power of His resurrection mean in your life?

Praise You, Father, for the resurrection! It changes everything. Not only have You redeemed us in Christ; You have also raised us up with Him. May I live each day by Your power, walking in the fullness of Jesus' resurrection life.

AMEN.

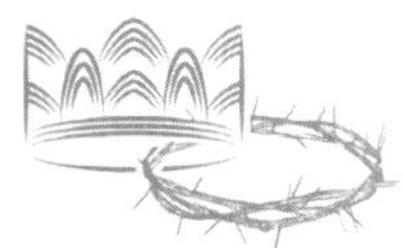

Day 44

Resurrection Revisited

The Calvary Miracles, Part 2

The tombs were also opened and many bodies of the saints who had fallen asleep were raised.

—MATTHEW 27:52

Do you sometimes wish you could know more about certain biblical events than what is revealed to us in Scripture? Matthew 27:52 records one such incident that piques my curiosity.

This brief verse tells us that people whose graves had flown open following the subterranean aftershocks of Christ's crucifixion suddenly began showing up in town. In person. Alive.

I can't help but wonder why this remarkable story would be given such scant attention in the narrative. All we get is a tiny slice of bare-bones reporting: "They came out of the tombs after his resurrection, entered the holy city, and appeared to many" (Matt. 27:53).

Dead people disinterred and walking around town? Surely such a miraculous moment calls for a little more elaboration!

But let's simply go where the biblical account leads us. These were "saints," the Bible says—literally, "holy ones," probably Old Testament believers who had died looking forward to and trusting in the redeeming work of Jesus the Messiah. After coming out of their tombs, they physically "appeared" to people, most likely to other believers, just as Jesus did following His own resurrection (1 Cor. 15:4–7). So there's *power* at work here. The power of God. The earthquakes that cracked these tombs open were not just random tremors. They clearly coincided with the spiritual convulsions of the crucifixion.

But beyond this extraordinary evidence of God's power, we see also signs of His *provision*. By multiplying the proof of what the resurrection represents, He gave Christ's followers exactly what He knew they would need in days to come, thus demonstrating His love and care for them.

Try putting yourself in the place of those early believers in the days following the resurrection. They'd allied themselves with a crucified carpenter who was now unbelievably alive. They'd placed themselves outside of the religious Jewish mainstream. Their belief in Jesus was soon to be greatly tested, and the suffering they'd be required to endure for Him would run the gamut from ferocious to fatal.

Imagine how the sight of these resurrected saints must have served to bolster their faith, to give them hope, and to remind them that

- Christ's death had truly put death to death.
- Christ was (and is) indeed the resurrection and the life.
- Christ was (is) the "firstfruits of those who have fallen asleep" (1 Cor. 15:20).
- Every person who dies in Him will be raised in Him, brought back from the dead to live with Him forever.

The community of early believers needed this visible, tangible encouragement of rubbing shoulders with resurrected saints as preparation for the challenges of faith that lay ahead for them. At any time in the future when their spiritual supplies were running low, they'd be able to look back and remember their interactions with the truly dead who were now truly alive.

They needed it. God knew they needed it. And God gave them what they needed.

God still—always—provides what His people need. And He will give you and me exactly what He knows we need, in preparation for every trial to our faith that lies ahead.

Let me suggest another important takeaway for our encouragement from this account recorded in Matthew's gospel: *perspective*.

The soldiers who witnessed the earthquake and the other wonders surrounding the crucifixion "were filled with awe" (Matt. 27:54 ESV). No doubt the same was true of those who encountered these newly resurrected saints. This was all so fresh and amazing to the participants in these world-changing events.

God's miraculous story is still being written today in us and in the lives of others around us who are coming to life by the power of the resurrected Christ.

Yet I'm struck by how easy it is for us to lose our sense of wonder over what took place on that historic weekend. Is it possible that His great, redeeming, life-giving works have become both too familiar and too distant in our eyes and hearts? Have we lost confidence in what He can do—what He is still doing today?

God's power to move heaven and earth, to awaken those who are spiritually dead, to bring them to life, grant forgiveness, and change the entire trajectory of people's lives, is no less a miracle than the earth quaking and all those saints coming out of their tombs in anticipation of Jesus' resurrection from the dead.

Charles Spurgeon said it like this:

> These first miracles wrought in connection with the death of Christ were typical of spiritual wonders that will be continued till He comes again—rocky hearts are rent, graves of sin are opened, those who have been dead in trespasses and sins and buried in sepulchers of lust and evil are quickened and come out from among the dead.[40]

Praise God, the resurrection story is not limited to a given historical moment. God's miraculous story is still being written today in us and in the lives of others around us who are coming to life by the power of the resurrected Christ. Opening our eyes and our hearts to that reality can energize our faith and renew our joy.

And here's one final takeaway from this intriguing little snippet of Scripture: not only does it remind us of God's *power,* His *provision,* and His gift of fresh *perspective;* it also provides the *promise* of resurrection miracles yet to come. Thinking of friends and loved ones who have died in the Lord, I find great joy in knowing that their souls are now in His presence. And that one day—the great Resurrection Day—their physical bodies will be raised and glorified. On that day you and I will also be raised to live forever with our resurrected Christ.

What a wonder this is! And what a triumph it will be.

How does the account of saints being raised from the dead following Christ's resurrection strengthen and encourage your faith?

How have you experienced the reality that "He gives us what we need"? Have you ever been surprised by the way He met your needs?

Father in heaven, thank You for knowing what we need—and supplying it. Thank You that You are still bringing dead souls to life. Thank You for the promise that one day my dead body will be raised in glory, never to die again. And in the meantime, thank You for the gift of daily hope through the resurrection life of Jesus within me.

AMEN.

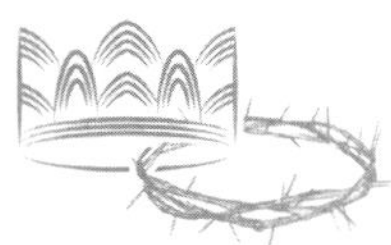

Day 45

Why Wait?

The Ministry of the Forty Days

He also presented himself alive to them by many convincing proofs, appearing to them over a period of forty days.

—ACTS 1:3

Thirty-three years is a long time to be away from home.

Imagine how eagerly Jesus wanted to get back to the heaven He'd come from. Back with the Father who loved Him. His work on earth was done: a perfect life, a prophetic death, a profoundly unprecedented resurrection from the grave. What could possibly be left for Him to do? Why must He wait in this wretched world for even a moment longer?

But Jesus did wait.

He delayed His departure from earth not just long enough to say His goodbyes, but for an extended forty-day interlude. Just shy of six weeks, which can seem like an eternity when you're longing for something that's already been years in the waiting.

This is part of what makes our Jesus incomparable, and it's why I wanted us to share these several more days together, beyond when many people end their celebration of Easter. Because this amazing story of the Word made flesh continues on beyond the cross and the resurrection.

Forty days. We've heard that before in biblical history. Think Noah's flood. Think Moses' stay on Mount Sinai and Jesus' temptation in the wilderness. The repetition of this time period tells us that it's significant. That the delay in Jesus' homecoming wasn't just an unexpected, last-minute change in travel plans, but a part of Jesus' divinely scheduled itinerary.

But again, why? Why not just be resurrected right up into heaven?

Well, obviously, Jesus stayed because the Father wanted Him to. The Son always does what the Father says. But Jesus wasn't just twiddling His thumbs during those forty days. His activity in that window of time not only encouraged those first-century followers but continues to bless us today.

Bear in mind that the disciples were likely confused, experiencing emotional whiplash with first the death and burial of their Leader and dearest Friend and then reports of His resurrection. The opening verses of the book of Acts reveal that Jesus used this brief period to reorient and care for His followers in at least two ways.

1. Jesus provided "many convincing proofs" of His resurrection (Acts 1:3).

He would soon be leaving them, and the whole future of His mission would depend on His followers having confidence that He had overcome the grave. If they were going to convince others, they needed to be sure themselves! So He presented them with evidence they couldn't refute—through multiple physical appearances intended to build their faith. They saw His glorified body. They touched Him. They ate and talked with Him. The evidence was indisputable and convincing—they could never doubt again.

Luke's account in Acts tells us that He showed Himself to them "after he had suffered" (v. 3)—a reminder that suffering and death are not final. They would suffer, too, for He had called them to take up their crosses and follow Him (Matt. 16:24). But the worst that could happen to them would be death, and Jesus was standing before them as evidence that there is life after death.

It's important to note that the evidence Jesus provided was not just for those first-generation disciples, but also for future generations of skeptics and believers alike. Even today, the eyewitness accounts of the resurrection remain compelling.

2. Jesus prepared His followers for what lay ahead after His departure.

He did this, first, by *teaching them.* Acts 1 tells us He gave "instructions through the Holy Spirit to the apostles he had chosen . . . speaking about the kingdom of God" (vv. 1, 3). These were subjects He'd likely talked about at length before but they hadn't fully understood or absorbed. Being taught by the risen Lord surely helped their comprehension this time around.

And note that Jesus purposefully pointed His followers to Scripture for what they needed to know. When He encountered two of them on the road to Emmaus, "beginning with Moses and all the Prophets, he interpreted for them the things concerning himself in all the Scriptures" (Luke 24:27). Later that same day, when He appeared to a group of disciples, "he opened their minds to understand the Scriptures" (v. 45).

You and I cannot see Jesus in the flesh. But what a great gift it is to have that same Word available to us and the same Holy Spirit to illumine our understanding and teach us what we need to know.

Jesus also prepared His followers by *confirming and clarifying their calling and mission.* They were not to just sit back after He left, reminisce about the good old days, and enjoy the blessings of their relationship with Him. No, He had a job for them to do: "As the Father has sent me, I also send you" (John 20:21)—to "make disciples of all nations" (Matt. 28:19). As "witnesses" (Luke 24:48) of His life, death, and resurrection, they were to proclaim the message of "repentance for forgiveness of sins" all over the world" (v. 47).

Jesus has left us with the same mission and message. He is coming back, as He promised. And He will hold us accountable for how well we've carried out our mandate in His absence.

Finally, during those forty days after the resurrection, Jesus prepared His disciples for the future by *assuring them of His provision.* The Roman government was big and powerful. How were they to fulfill this mission to proclaim His kingdom?

In the final hours before His crucifixion, He had promised His disciples that the Father would send them a "Helper" after He returned to heaven (John 14:26 NKJV). Now He reminded them of that promise: "You will receive power when the Holy Spirit has come on you, and you will be my witnesses" (Acts 1:8).

The coming of the Spirit—their empowering, encouraging Guide—meant that Jesus would always be with them, as He is with us. Christ has given us every resource we need to fulfill His mission in this world through His Holy Spirit and His presence in and among us. What more could we ask?

Jesus could have gone on to His Father and left His followers to figure everything out on their own. But He cared more about them (and about us) than He cared about Himself. He cared more about preparing them for what was to come than He cared about returning to heaven. He cared more about completing His Father's agenda than about rushing home to celebrate His victory.

So He waited—and how grateful we should be that He did.

What are one or two blessings from Jesus' final forty days on earth for which you're especially grateful?

Do you sometimes feel impatient to enjoy the glory that awaits you in heaven? How can Jesus' example encourage you while you wait?

Thank You, Father, that Jesus waited here on earth for those final forty days to encourage, equip, and prepare His disciples—including us—to take the gospel into the world. May we be faithful to our mission, as He was to His, until it's Your time to take us home.

AMEN.

Day 46

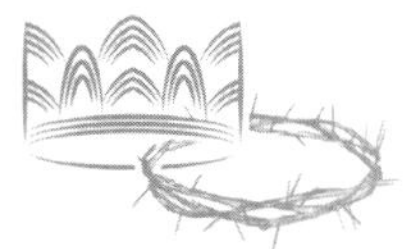

All the Way Home

The Ascension of Christ

"What if you were to observe the Son of Man ascending to where he was before?"
—JOHN 6:62

A footnote. An epilogue. An interesting little postscript to the main story. That's the way many people think of Jesus' ascension into heaven.

But just as He had plainly predicted His death and resurrection, Jesus had also made clear what would follow. "I am only with you for a short time," He'd told His disciples. He would soon be leaving—and not just going away, but going home: "I came from the Father and have come into the world. Again, I am leaving the world and going to the Father" (John 16:28).

The ascension was all part of the plan, in other words. It was not some sort of theatrical device, a clever solution to the problem of getting Him off the stage. Nor was it a minor blip on the salvation calendar. It was a vital event, essential to the Christian faith, with momentous implications for our lives as believers.

Think of the alternative. What if Jesus had just vanished? What if His disciples had gone looking for Him one day and He was nowhere to be found? What would that have done to the confidence He'd worked so hard to instill in His followers if the only thing they could conclusively say about their resurrected Lord was that He'd turned up missing?

No, the ascension needed to happen exactly the way it did.

First, *it needed to be visible.* "He was taken up as they were watching,"

Acts 1:9 tells us. There were eyewitnesses who saw Him lifted up bodily into the heavens. The event was stunning, yes, and unexpected, but unforgettable. The disciples would always remember the day He "led them out to the vicinity of Bethany," a little town just outside Jerusalem, and "left them" (Luke 24:50–51).

In addition, *Jesus' exit from the world needed to be physical.* He had come to the earth in human flesh. Now He was leaving the earth in human flesh. The ministry He'd conducted while walking around physically on this planet was completed, with the ascension marking His departure in a dramatic way. The people who saw Him leave saw the Jesus they'd always known.

Jesus' glorious bodily ascension to His Father in heaven comes with the promise that He'll return one day, visibly and bodily, to reclaim us so we can follow Him where He's gone—to a physical heaven and to a personal God.

And here's an important fact that's often overlooked: *Jesus didn't just dissolve or disappear when He ascended to heaven.* He didn't shed His physical body or stop being a man. No, He remained incarnate. He would continue His eternal ministry from heaven *while retaining His human body*—a glorified body, yet still a recognizable, human one.

On the eve of His crucifixion, Jesus had prayed to His Father: "I have glorified you on the earth by completing the work you gave me to do. Now, Father, glorify me in your presence with that glory I had with you before the world existed" (John 17:4–5). And the manner of His departure showed that His prayer had been answered.

In Acts 1:9 we are told that as He ascended "a cloud took him out of their sight." That's a significant detail because clouds in Scripture symbolize the presence and glory of God. Remember the cloud that rested on Mount Sinai at the giving of the Ten Commandments (Ex. 19:16)? Remember the "pillar of cloud" that guided the Israelites in their travels (Ex. 13:21), protected them from Egyptian soldiers at the Red Sea (Ex. 14:19), and hovered above the tabernacle where they worshiped in the wilderness (Num. 9:15)? The cloud that billowed around the Son at His ascension indicated that He was being transported into His Father's presence, not into some unknown portal, never to be seen again.

In fact, two men—two angels—suddenly appeared alongside the cluster of Christ's followers watching Him ascend and reminded them that there was more to the story:

> "Why do you stand looking up into heaven? This same Jesus, who has been taken from you into heaven, will come in the same way that you have seen him going into heaven." (Acts 1:11)

That word is for us, too, as we contemplate what happened that day. Jesus' glorious bodily ascension to His Father in heaven comes with the promise that He'll return one day, visibly and bodily, to reclaim us so we can follow Him where He's gone—to a physical heaven and to a personal God. We are guaranteed by His grace that we will appear in His presence in new, glorified bodies. The redemptive path that leads us there was paved not only by His death and resurrection but also by His return to heaven.

The ascension of Christ is meant to give us confidence and courage. To neglect it as a key component in our faith is to stop short of experiencing the full purpose and promise—and the blessings—of His incarnation.

The ascension account recorded in Luke's gospel includes one further detail I don't want you to miss. We read that when they arrived at the place where He would depart from them, Jesus lifted up His hands and "*blessed them*. And while he was blessing them, he left them and was carried up to heaven" (Luke 24:50–51). Jesus had blessed His followers while He was here on earth. Now, as He was leaving them, He blessed them once again. (In the next devotion we'll see how He is still blessing them—and us!—today in heaven.)

Luke's gospel ends by telling us that the disciples "returned to Jerusalem with great joy, and were continually in the temple *blessing God*" (vv. 52–53 ESV). Jesus' final earthly blessing broke through the sorrow they had experienced at the prospect of their Friend leaving. It filled them with joy, and they could not stop blessing Him in return.

Truly, the ascension is accompanied by blessings abounding eternally—from our resurrected Savior to us and from our hearts back to Him.

What does it tell you about Jesus that in heaven He retains a human body like ours? What does it tell you about your physical body?

How does Jesus' ascension into heaven give you hope and assurance about your future?

Father, You see all things through to their completion. You leave nothing undone. Your great work of redemption is not a temporary phase of Your Son's life but an unbroken line extending into eternity. May the wonder of the ascension fill our hearts with hope and joy as we await His return to earth to take those who belong to You to live with You in heaven forever.

AMEN.

Day 47

Seated with Him

The Exaltation of Christ

He humbled himself by becoming obedient
to the point of death—
even to death on a cross.
For this reason God highly exalted him
and gave him the name
that is above every name.
—PHILIPPIANS 2:8–9

Peering through the picturesque language of these two verses from Philippians, we're given a slightly different angle on the moment when Jesus relocated His theater of operations from earth to heaven. The ascension marks a seamless dividing line in this passage. Somewhere in the clouds above that Judean hillside, the humiliation the Son of God experienced by choosing to walk among us on earth and to die on a cross gave way to the supreme exaltation He experiences now and for all eternity.

But what happened next, after He disappeared into the clouds, away from view of the disciples left standing on the hillside? By piecing together other Scriptures, you and I can enjoy brief glimpses of some of the events that followed His arrival in heaven as the exalted, returning Christ.

First, Scripture tells us that *He "sat down at the right hand of the Majesty on high"* (Heb. 1:3). This is the posture of a conquering hero, resting securely in the work He'd accomplished. Now, don't confuse sitting with being sedentary! Jesus remained (and remains) highly active upon that throne. But the completeness and certainty of His kingly reign, though it awaits its fullness at the end of time, has given Him the right to take His seat at the Father's side, where He lives and serves today.

This is not just an interesting theological tidbit. It is hugely significant for your life and mine down here on earth. You see, Scripture calls us to identify with Jesus at each point of His redemptive work.

Concerning His crucifixion, for example: "We have been united with him in the likeness of his death. . . . Our old self was crucified with him" (Rom. 6:5–6). But we haven't just been crucified with Him. We are also "united with Him . . . in the likeness of his resurrection (vv. 5–6). We can "consider [ourselves] dead to sin and alive to God in Christ Jesus" (v. 11). Crucified with Him, made alive with Him.

Beyond that, *we are also united with Him in His exalted place at the right hand of the Father.* Ephesians 2 tells us that God "seated us with him in the heavens in Christ Jesus" (v. 6). Think about that. Positionally, you and I are seated there with Jesus right now. So as we start each day, facing whatever temptations and challenges may rise to greet us, we don't fight from a point of defeat and deficiency. When life here on earth feels overwhelming, let's remember where we're seated. With Christ. In heaven. Victorious because of the victory He has already won.

So the crucified, risen Christ is seated next to the Father in heaven. By faith, we are seated there with Him. And that's not all. Let's look at what happened after Jesus ascended and took His seat on the throne. *He received glory, honor, and authority.* "Angels, authorities, and powers" were all made "subject to him" (1 Peter 3:22). In fact, the Father "appointed him as head over everything for the church" (Eph. 1:22). Everything! And Jesus graciously allows us to participate in this aspect of His reign as well.

Our being "in Christ" means He has given us the right as believers "to sit with me on my throne, just as I also conquered and sat down with my Father on his throne" (Rev. 3:21). As His representatives here on earth, we share in the authority that has been given to Him. We engage in spiritual warfare from that position. And in the age to come, we will share in that position even more fully as we reign and rule with Him over His creation, over angels, and over the nations. We will reign with Him who reigns forever.

And as if that weren't enough, there's still more! To help us live out that lofty status, *the ascended Christ has given us the gift of the Holy Spirit*. As Peter explained to the bewildered crowds at Pentecost, "Since he [Jesus] has been exalted to the right hand of God and has received from the Father the promised Holy Spirit, he has poured out what you both see and hear" (Acts 2:33). This wouldn't have happened if Jesus had not ascended! If He had not been exalted in glory, we would not experience His indwelling life, heart, and power.

The crucified, risen Christ is seated next to the Father in heaven. By faith, we are seated there with Him.

When Jesus left the earth, the Bible says, He "took the captives captive" (Eph. 4:8). At the cross He conquered His enemies—Satan, demons, death, and all the spiritual forces of evil. Then, like a military commander returning in triumph with the plunder of war, "he gave gifts" (v. 8) to His people—sinners He'd rescued from Satan's control.

Those gifts are intended to equip His church for carrying out His ongoing redemptive mission in the world. They include the personal gift of His Spirit to encourage and counsel us, the plentiful gifts of His Spirit for us to employ in His service, and gifted leaders to serve the church (see Eph. 4:11).

As a result, everything about our life on earth is different now. Everything is better because Jesus has gone home to be exalted by the Father. By virtue of our union with Him, we are raised and seated with Him, serving with Him to fulfill His kingdom purposes in our world, through the enabling of His Holy Spirit who is powerfully at work in and through us.

Praise be to our risen, ascended Christ, from whom all blessings flow.

What does it mean to you as a Christ follower to know that you have been raised and are seated with Him in heaven?

How does Christ's exalted position in heaven equip and enable you to serve Him and others in this world?

Lord Jesus, You came here to save us, but You have gone away to bless us and to receive the worship due You as the eternal King of glory. What a wonder that You have secured my redemption, that I am seated with You in heaven, and that You have given me all I need to serve You here on earth until faith becomes sight and I join You—body, soul, and spirit—in that holy place. I exalt You and bless Your name today and forever.

AMEN.

Day 48

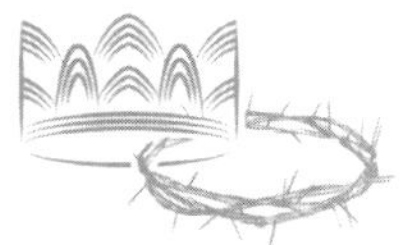

An Unchanging Priesthood

The Ongoing Work of Christ, Part 1

Because he remains forever, he holds his priesthood permanently.
—HEBREWS 7:24

Let's face it—change is a given in our lives. And most of us, if we're honest, don't love change, especially if we didn't choose it. If we were sitting across from each other today, we'd probably have no trouble recalling the drastic changes our world has endured in recent years and how challenging they've been to deal with. We might also talk about unwanted change in more personal areas of our lives: our health, work, finances, and families.

Our Father knows all this. He knows the burden of stress we carry from the uncertainty that never stops swirling around us—confusing, overwhelming, and upsetting us. And in His mercy and love He's chosen to lift this burden from us—not by eliminating change from our lives, but by giving us Jesus as *our unchanging constant*: "the same yesterday, today, and forever" (Heb. 13:8).

Jesus is our fixed anchor in a constantly changing world. But we may think of this mostly in terms of His presence when He was here on the earth—we know that He died on the cross, rose from the grave, and ascended to heaven. We also know that He promised to return one day in the future and take us to be with Him. But what is He doing in the meantime? How is He a constant presence and help in our lives right now?

Sadly, many Christians live without conscious recognition of or dependence on a living, active Savior. That means they are missing out on an incredible resource. In this reading and the next, I want to invite you to meditate with me on how Jesus serves and blesses us today and every day in His role as our faithful and eternal High Priest.

Throughout the Old Testament, the high priest performed two vital roles on behalf of believers: service *to* God and service *from* God. By carrying the sacrificial blood of an animal into the holy of holies—that most sacred place in the temple, where Yahweh's presence dwelt—the high priest represented the people to God, seeking atonement for their sins. Then, emerging from that sanctuary, having had the sacrifice accepted, he represented God to the people, offering them divine pardon, peace, and blessing.

But powerful and holy as this service was, the high priest's ministry was inherently limited. Though bearing the sins of the people, he also bore the guilt of his own sins. Plus, he could only serve a finite number of years, depending on how long he lived. Like those he served, he aged and eventually died. Even in faithfully carrying out his duties, in the end he represented one more unwelcome change in people's lives.

But not Jesus. Never Jesus. He solved each of the inevitable flaws and weaknesses in the priestly system by entering "into heaven itself, so that he may now appear in the presence of God for us" (Heb. 9:24). And as Hebrews 7:26–28 assures us,

> This is the kind of high priest we need: holy, innocent, undefiled, separated from sinners, and exalted above the heavens. He doesn't need to offer sacrifices every day, as high priests do—first for their own sins, then for those of the people. He did this once for all time when he offered himself. For the law appoints as high priests men who are weak, but the promise of the oath, which came after the law, appoints a Son, who has been perfected forever.

So not only did Jesus die on our behalf, becoming the sufficient sacrifice for our sins. In His ascension He also took that offering into the true holy of holies in heaven (Heb 9:24). He presented to the Father His pure, perfect life and the blood that He shed for our sin on Calvary, ending the need for anyone else to perform this service for His people ever again.

> He did not do this to offer himself many times, as the high priest enters the sanctuary yearly with the blood of another. Otherwise, he would have had to suffer many times since the foundation of the world. But now he has appeared one time, at the end of the ages, for the removal of sin by the sacrifice of himself. (Heb. 9:25–26)

Permanently. Unchangingly.

It is done. It is finished.

Jesus is our fixed anchor in a constantly changing world.

So let the world keep surprising us each morning with wild swings in the stock market, with unpredictable surges in contagious infections, with new political hot buttons and election issues, with technological developments that, in spite of their benefits, can also make our lives harder to understand and navigate. The constancy of change is an unavoidable reality that each of us has to live with. But we can find comfort and stability in the fact that

> we have a great high priest who has passed through the heavens—Jesus the Son of God. . . . For we do not have a high priest who is unable to sympathize with our weaknesses, but one who has been tempted in every way as we are, yet without sin. Therefore, let us approach the throne of grace with boldness, so that we may receive mercy and find grace to help us in time of need. (Heb. 4:14–16)

In times of elevated concerns and disruptive changes, our great High Priest is not going anywhere. And today, in heaven, He continues to serve us, representing us to the Father when we confess our sins, and representing the Father to us by granting us the mercy and grace we need—all through the sufficient sacrifice He made for us on the cross, once for all.

How can an awareness of Christ's constancy help you respond to unwanted changes in our world and in your life?

How does the ongoing priestly ministry of Christ make a difference in your life?

Father, thank You that in Christ I have a sinless, unchanging High Priest in heaven. Thank You for accepting His sacrifice for my sin. And thank You that I have been granted permanent access into Your presence through His ongoing priestly ministry on my behalf. Hallelujah!

AMEN.

Day 49

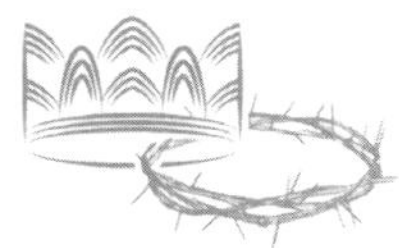

The One We Need Today

The Ongoing Work of Christ, Part 2

Christ has appeared as a high priest of
the good things that have come.
—HEBREWS 9:11

Do you ever feel stuck and stagnant in your spiritual life? No doubt, we all experience this at times. And one of the reasons it happens, I believe, is that we lose sight of what Jesus is doing for us—right now, today—from His exalted seat in heaven.

We know, for example, that

- *He is preparing a place for us.* We don't know exactly what this "place" will be like, but if Jesus is the One getting it ready for us (as He promises in John 14:2), it must be wonderful beyond description.
- *He is enjoying close and loving fellowship with His Father.* And we believers, whom the Bible says are "hidden with Christ in God" (Col. 3:3), are mystically included with Him in this eternal circle of relationship.
- *He is leading His church.* As the reigning "head of the body" (Col. 1:18), He is walking "among the lampstands" (Rev. 1:13) in full power and authority, protecting and purifying His people as we represent and serve Him here on earth.

It's important to remember that Jesus is not a distant, faraway ruler periodically glancing down on us from heaven with no real connection to what we're experiencing here on earth. He is active and engaged—observing, guiding, supplying, providing. And in His high priestly role, which He perfectly and permanently carried out by His sacrifice for our sins, He continues to serve us every day and to meet the deepest needs of our hearts.

How does He do that? For starters, Jesus is our *Mediator* with the Father. A mediator is someone who intervenes between two disputing parties. And make no mistake, we entered this life in the middle of an irreconcilable dispute with God. As sinners, in fact, we were His "enemies" (Rom. 5:10).

Ours is not a past-tense Savior. He's not left us here to languish until He finally chooses to rescue us from this earthly mess and whisk us away to heaven. Jesus is working now.

But there is a hope—and only *one* hope: "One mediator between God and mankind, the man Christ Jesus" (1 Tim. 2:5). Jesus alone can resolve the dispute that exists between us and the Father. He who "gave himself as a ransom for all" (v. 6) is uniquely qualified, as both God and man, to be the Mediator we so desperately need.

But He not only mediated for us by bridging this impossible divide between us and the Father. He *continues* mediating for us today when, even as believers, we choose distance from God rather than peace with God. Jesus remains our righteousness, our one and only Mediator, the source of our salvation, and the only way for us to be restored to unbroken fellowship with God.

Jesus is also our *Advocate* with the Father. Our shame and guilt can be relentless accusers, goaded on by Satan himself,

> the accuser of our brothers and sisters,
> who accuses them
> before our God day and night. (Rev. 12:10)

If we had no sin, of course, if there was nothing that either he or we could hold up as evidence to substantiate such accusations, we could shrug them off as having no merit. But we *have* sinned, and we *do* sin, despite being shown the way in Scripture and daily empowered by the Spirit to keep from sin. Yet God's Word assures us that "if anyone does sin, we have an advocate with the Father—Jesus Christ the righteous one" (1 John 2:1), who continually serves as our defense attorney, arguing our case before the Father. His appeal is not for clemency, asking God to withhold rightful punishment against sins deserving of judgment. Christ's advocacy for us is an appeal for justice based on the fact that "He himself is the atoning sacrifice for our sins" (v. 2). Yes, we *ought* to die for our sins—but Jesus has already died for our sins. Our penalty is paid. Our record is clear. And our Advocate will never stop winning this case for us.

Beyond all of this, Jesus *makes intercession for us* to the Father. I think of Him mediating; I think of Him advocating. And how very much we need Him for these things. Yet what could be more precious and personal to you and me than thinking of Jesus in heaven praying for us, pleading for us, interceding for us.

"Who is the one who condemns? Christ Jesus is the one who died, but even more, has been raised; he also is at the right hand of God and intercedes for us" (Rom. 8:34)—in fact, "*lives* to intercede" for us (Heb. 7:25). When we fail, when we struggle, when we doubt, when we're in need, our High Priest Himself, who offered His life for our sins, is *always* praying for us. And because He lives to intercede for us, we will never encounter a day that we cannot endure.

As Oswald Sanders wrote:

> There is no personal problem for which He has no solution, no enemy from whom He cannot rescue, no sin from which He cannot deliver—because He ever lives to make intercession for us.[41]

Ours is not a past-tense Savior. He's not left us here to languish until He finally chooses to rescue us from this earthly mess and whisk us away to heaven. Jesus is working now. He is working at this hour. Working for you, working for me. Doing what we need, what no one else could ever do for us.

How would our lives be different if Jesus were disengaged, unavailable, and inattentive to our needs?

In what areas do you most depend on His advocacy and intercession today? How are you helped and encouraged knowing He is actively defending and praying for you?

Thank You, Lord, that at this moment in heaven, I have a Mediator. At this moment, I have an Advocate. At this moment, I am benefiting from a ministry of intercession conducted by One who is pleading and fighting for me more earnestly and effectively than I could ever plead or fight for myself. Thank You, Lord Jesus, for never giving up on me, for never ceasing to work on my behalf. I need You, and I love You.

AMEN.

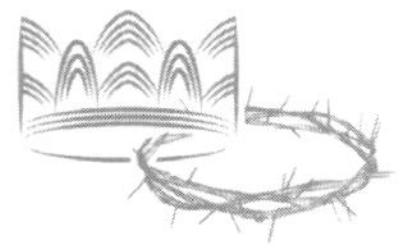

Day 50

Until He Comes

The Second Advent of Christ

"This same Jesus, who has been taken from you into heaven, will come in the same way that you have seen him going into heaven."

—ACTS 1:11

We've come to the close of our reflections on the incomparable Jesus. My hope is that you have come to know Him more personally, trust Him more deeply, worship Him more sincerely, and love Him more fervently. And as we come to this final reading, I pray you will be moved to anticipate more eagerly all that He still has in store for us.

We've seen Him preexistent. We've seen Him incarnate. We've seen Him as a child and as a man. We've seen Him live . . . and die . . . and live again. And we've seen Him taken up to live forever with the Father in heaven, where He advocates and intercedes for us. Our portrait of Jesus is nearly—but not quite—complete. The capstone, the crowning point of Christ's life is still in the future.

His second coming.

When Gen. Douglas MacArthur was forced to leave the Philippines in the early part of World War II to escape the Japanese offensive, he made a short speech, which ended with the phrase for which he is best known: "I shall return." More than two years later, Gen. MacArthur fulfilled his promise, returning to the Philippines in victory.

Two thousand years ago, the Lord Jesus, the great General of our faith, left this world in the midst of a hotly contested battle. When He left, He also promised: "I shall return." This hope of a "second advent"[42] sustained those first-century believers through intense threats and persecutions, and generations of Christ followers since then have found courage and comfort in Christ's promise that "I am coming soon" (Rev. 20:22), even (especially!) when it seemed the enemy was making great gains.

We don't know precisely when our Savior will return (Matt. 24:36), but we know that day is coming, and we know it will be glorious!

As we wrap up our time together, let's consider how Jesus' second advent will differ from His first:

- He arrived on earth the first time as an infant, born in time and space, small and weak. He will return as the everlasting King, mighty in strength and glory.
- When He came the first time, He shrouded and concealed His glory. When He comes the second time, His glory will shine out brightly.
- His first coming was obscure, witnessed only by His earthly parents, some farm animals, and a few poor shepherds, with almost no one recognizing who He was. At His second coming, every eye will see Him and know exactly who He is.
- At His first coming He was judged and condemned to die by sinful people. When He returns, He will come as Judge to execute justice and judgment on all people who have refused to repent of their sins.
- He came the first time as a Man of Sorrows. He will return the second time as almighty God.
- At His first advent He rode into Jerusalem on a lowly donkey. When He returns, He will be riding a majestic white horse.
- When He came the first time, only a few people knelt to pay Him homage. When He returns, every knee will bow and every tongue confess that He is Lord.

- He came the first time to die. The second time He will come to reign.
- The first time He came as a humble servant. The second time He will come as Commander in Chief of the armies of heaven.
- The first time He came to wear a crown of thorns. When He returns, He will be crowned with many crowns.
- He came the first time to make peace between God and man. When He returns, He will make war on those who have rebelled against Him.
- He came the first time as our suffering Savior. He will return as our sovereign, ruling Lord.

Oh, what a day that will be. How my heart longs for His return. Doesn't yours? But how are we to live in the meantime, when His return seems so far off that we can easily lose sight of it altogether?

God's Word gives us clear marching orders as we await the fulfillment of His promise. We are urged

- to be alert and watchful, eagerly awaiting His return, which could be at any moment (2 Peter 3:12–13)
- to keep our hearts detached from this world (2 Tim. 4:8)
- to make every effort to live holy lives (1 John 3:3)
- to serve Him zealously and faithfully until He returns (Luke 12:43)

We don't know precisely when our Savior will return, but we know that day is coming, and we know it will be glorious!

The "blessed hope" of Christ's return (Titus 2:13) will strengthen and carry you and me through every wearisome day of this life, for "now our salvation is nearer than when we first believed" (Rom. 13:11).

In the meantime, "based on his promise," let us patiently "wait for new heavens and a new earth, where righteousness dwells" (2 Peter 3:13). Then we will see His face, and there we will worship and serve Him forever.

Our Jesus.

Our *incomparable* Jesus.

Read Revelation 11:15 and ponder its triumphant words. What are you especially looking forward to about that day when the "kingdom of the world" becomes the kingdom "of our Lord and of his Christ"?

The Bible urges us to "encourage one another" with reminders that Christ is coming again (1 Thess. 4:18). Who could you bless today by sharing this wonderful promise?

Lord, You are truly beyond compare. You bless us from beginning to end, loving and providing for us in every way. You assure us with Your mercy, just as You astound us with Your power. Thank You for coming to us and making Yourself known to us. Use my life, I pray, to make Your greatness known to others that they, too, may see, believe, and worship.

AMEN.

Heartfelt Gratitude

As is always the case, multiple friends and colleagues have journeyed with me in the writing of the book you hold in your hands. And, as usual, the path has been longer and more taxing at times than most of us originally anticipated, but there have been joys aplenty along the way. My heart is full of gratitude for each one who has helped make it possible for you to spend these "fifty days with Jesus." Among them . . .

Lawrence Kimbrough skillfully organized and drafted the content from my teaching on this subject and **Anne Christian Buchanan** patiently worked with me through one round after another (and another!) of painstaking edits. These two are an author's dream team. They are humble, gifted servants who know and love the Scripture well and whose fingerprints are on each page of this book. They deserve far more recognition and applause than they will get this side of heaven. But the One who keeps track of these things knows, and He will reward them. I could not be more thankful for their tireless, glad-hearted labors.

Dr. Chris Cowan kindly reviewed dozens of specific questions to ensure biblical and theological soundness. His thoughtful, careful input has been invaluable.

If I'm counting correctly, this is the twenty-third book the **Moody Publishers** team and I have worked on together in as many years. How blessed I've been to serve alongside these friends. When we first ventured out together, we could not have imagined all the fruit He would bring about through this ministry partnership.

The quiet, behind-the-scenes efforts of my agent, **Erik Wolgemuth**, have kept all of us moving in the same direction and helped us arrive at the destination together. What a gift you are, Erik.

My precious husband, **Robert Wolgemuth** . . . what can I say? Your encouragement, wisdom, love, and prayers mean more than you could possibly know. I love you so.

Finally, to my incomparable **Lord Jesus**:

You are fairer than the sons of men;
Grace is poured upon Your lips;
Therefore God has blessed You forever.
Gird Your sword upon Your thigh, O Mighty One,
With Your glory and Your majesty.
And in Your majesty ride prosperously
because of truth, humility, and righteousness.
(Ps. 45:2–4 NKJV)

My beloved is . . . Chief among ten thousand. . . .
His mouth is most sweet,
Yes, he is altogether lovely.
This is my beloved,
And this is my friend.
(Song of Songs 5:10, 16 NKJV)

Other Books from Nancy DeMoss Wolgemuth and Moody Publishers

A 30-Day Walk with God in the Psalms

A Place of Quiet Rest: Cultivating Intimacy with God through a Daily Devotional Life

Adorned: Living Out the Beauty of the Gospel Together

Born a Child and Yet a King: The Gospel in the Carols: A 31-Day Advent Devotional

Brokenness, Holiness, Surrender: A Revive Our Hearts Trilogy

Choosing Forgiveness: Moving from Hurt to Hope

Choosing Gratitude: Your Journey to Joy

Heaven Rules: Take Courage. Take Comfort. Our God is in Control.

Lies Women Believe: And the Truth That Sets Them Free

Lies Young Women Believe: And the Truth That Sets Them Free (Dannah Gresh, coauthor)

Seeking Him: Experiencing the Joy of Personal Revival (Tim Grissom, coauthor)

The First Songs of Christmas: Meditations on Luke 1 & 2: A 31-Day Advent Devotional

The Quiet Place: Daily Devotional Readings

The Wonder of His Name: 32 Life-Changing Names of Jesus

True Woman 101: Divine Design (Mary Kassian, coauthor)

True Woman 201: Interior Design (Mary Kassian, coauthor)

You Can Trust God to Write Your Story: Embracing the Mysteries of Providence (Robert Wolgemuth, coauthor)

Voices of the True Woman Movement: A Call to the Counter-Revolution

Notes

1. Samuel Stennett, "Majestic Sweetness Sits Enthroned," 1787, www.hymnal.net/en/hymn/h/177.

2. Isaac Ambrose, *Looking unto Jesus: A View of the Everlasting Gospel; or, The Soul's Eying of Jesus, as Carrying on the Great Work of Man's Salvation, from First to Last* (Glasgow: John Knox, 1758), vi.

3. John Stott, *The Radical Disciple: Some Neglected Aspects of Our Calling* (Downers Grove, IL: InterVarsity, 2010), 20.

4. First published in 1925, the book is still in print as a Moody Classics edition: Oswald Sanders, *The Incomparable Christ*, Moody Classics (Chicago: Moody Publishers, 2009).

5. S. M. Lockridge (1913–2000), "That's My King," from a sermon delivered many times, many places, and in many versions. This one from 1976 is quoted in Justin Taylor, "Well, I Wonder If You Know Him," blog, The Gospel Coalition, April 9, 2009, https://www.thegospelcoalition.org/blogs/justin-taylor/well-i-wonder-if-you-know-him/.

6. John Flavel, "Christ Altogether Lovely," SermonIndex.net, www.sermonindex.net/modules/articles/index.php?view=article&aid=2927.

7. Wayne Grudem, *Systematic Theology: An Introduction to Biblical Doctrine*, 2nd ed. (Grand Rapids, MI: Zondervan Academic, 2020), 700.

8. *The Infancy Gospel of Thomas*, in *The Apocryphal New Testament: A Collection of Apocryphal Christian Literature in an English Translation based on M. R. James*, ed. J. K. Elliott (New York: Oxford University Press, 1993), 68–83. You can read M. R. James' 1924 translation at www.gnosis.org/library/inftoma.htm.

9. G. Campbell Morgan, *The Gospel According to Luke*, G. Campbell Morgan Reprint Series (Eugene, OR: Wipf and Stock, 1931, 2010), 46 (Luke 2:40–52).

10. J. Oswald Sanders, *The Incomparable Christ*, Moody Classics (Chicago: Moody Publishers, 2009), 70.

11. Matthew Vanatta, "Books That Have Sold Over 50 Million Copies," Stacker, August 1, 2019, https://stacker.com/stories/204/books-have-sold-over-50-million-copies.

12. Dan Brown, *The Da Vinci Code* (New York: Doubleday, 2003), 233.

13. Arthur W. Pink, *Gleanings in the Godhead* (Chicago: Moody Press, 1975), 149.

14. David Mathis, "His Scars Will Never Fade: The Wounds Christ Took to Heaven," Desiring God, May 18, 2019, https://www.desiringgod.org/articles/his-scars-will-never-fade. See also Randy Alcorn, "Why Does Jesus Have Scars on His Resurrection Body? Will They Be Permanent?," Eternal Perspective Ministries, June 18, 2020, www.epm.org/resources/2020/Jun/18/Jesus-scars-resurrection.

15. Matt Perman, "How Can Jesus Be God and Man?," Desiring God, October 5, 2006, www.desiringgod.org/articles/how-can-jesus-be-god-and-man.

16. Cultural Research Center, "American Worldview Inventory 2020—At a Glance," Arizona Christian University, April 21, 2020, https://www.arizonachristian.edu/wp-content/uploads/2020/04/CRC-AWVI-2020-Release-03_Perceptions-of-God.pdf.

17. Andrew Murray, *Humility: The Beauty of Holiness* (London: James Nisbet & Co., 1896), 12.

18. Sanders, *Incomparable Christ*, 186.

19. James Stalker, *Pulpit Legends: Studies on the Person of Christ* (Chattanooga, TN: AMG Publishers, 1995), 194–95.

20. *Passion* is a term traditionally used to refer to the suffering and death of our Savior.

21. John Piper, *Don't Waste Your Life* (Wheaton, IL: Crossway, 2003), 40.

22. Spiros Zodhiates, *The Complete Word Study: New Testament* (Chattanooga, TN: AMG Publishers, 1991), 868.

23. David Harsha, *The Star of Bethlehem: A Guide to the Savior* (Argyle, NY: 1863), chapter 6, "The Crucifixion," accessed at Grace Gems, www.gracegems.org/BOOKS/star06.htm.

24. Matthew Henry, *Matthew Henry's Commentary on the Whole Bible*, vol. 5, Matthew to John (Old Tappan, NJ: Revell, n.d., originally published 1896), 826.

25. The disciple "Jesus loved" is mentioned five times in the gospel of John (and only in that gospel)—13:23, 19:26, 20:2, 21:7, 21:20. Though Scripture never identifies this disciple by name, from earliest church tradition he has consistently been believed to be the apostle John, son of Zebedee, brother of James, and the author of the gospel of John and Revelation.

26. These times are based on gospel accounts that Jesus was crucified at the "third hour," that darkness descended at the "sixth hour," and that He died at around the "ninth hour" (Mark 15:25–34; Matthew 27:45; Luke 23:44). These times correspond approximately to nine a.m., twelve noon, and three p.m. But keep in mind that time references in the Gospels are not necessarily precise. (People didn't wear watches then!) The "third hour" probably refers to the quarter of a day surrounding nine a.m.—in other words, midmorning—and the other events described happened around noon and in midafternoon. For more on this, see Andres J. Köstenberger and Justin Taylor, *The Final Days of Jesus: The Most Important Person Who Ever Lived* (Wheaton, IL: Crossway, 2014), 142–43.
27. William Barclay, *Barclay's Daily Study Bible*, ch. 18, commentary on John 18:1–11, StudyLight, https://www.studylight.org/commentaries/eng/dsb/john-18.html.
28. Elizabeth Barrett Browning, "Cowper's Grave," in *The Seraphim, and Other Poems* (London: Saunders and Otley, 1838), 352.
29. Charles H. Spurgeon, "Psalm 22," in *The Treasury of David*, The Spurgeon Archive, https://archive.spurgeon.org/treasury/ps022.php.
30. The man said to have made this statement was Cecil Rhodes, a "financier, statesman, and empire builder of British South Africa." The South African state of Rhodesia—now the countries of Zimbabwe and Zambia—was named after him, as was the Rhodes scholarship. (See "Cecil Rhodes Summary," *Encyclopedia Britannica*, www.britannica.com/summary/Cecil-Rhodes.) Quotation is from Lewis Michell, *Life of Rhodes* (1910), vol. 2, ch. 39, quoted in *Oxford Essential Quotations*, ed. Susan Ratcliffe, 5th ed. (2017), Oxford Reference, www.oxfordreference.com/display/10.1093/acref/9780191843730.001.0001/q-oro-ed5-00008802;jsessionid=43E9C7BB23A1E3076567F28A4E8B64BA.
31. Ray Pritchard, "The Meaning of Tetelestai—'It Is Finished,'" Christianity.com, January 17, 2022, https://www.christianity.com/jesus/death-and-resurrection/last-words/what-was-finished.html.
32. *Vine's Expository Dictionary of New Testament Words*, s.v. "Strong's G5055 *teleo*," Blue Letter Bible, www.blueletterbible.org/search/dictionary/viewtopic.cfm?topic=VT0000021.
33. Frederick W. Krummacher, *The Suffering Saviour; or, A Series of Devotional Meditations*, tr. Samuel Jackson (Boston: Gould and Lincoln, 1856), 428–29. I recommend the reprint edition published by Banner of Truth Trust (2004).

34. Charles H. Spurgeon, "Christ's Dying Word for His Church," sermon delivered November 3, 1889, *Metropolitan Tabernacle Pulpit Volume 40,* Spurgeon Center for Biblical Preaching at Midwestern Seminary, www.spurgeon.org/resource-library/sermons/christs-dying-word-for-his-church/#flipbook.

35. Charles Wesley, "Christ the Lord Is Risen Today," 1739, Hymnary.org, https://hymnary.org/text/christ_the_lord_is_risen_today_wesley.

36. F. B. Meyer, *Love to the Uttermost,* quoted in Sanders, *Incomparable Christ,* 295.

37. Charles Wesley, "Love's Redeeming Work Is Done," Hymnary.org, https://hymnary.org/text/loves_redeeming_work_is_done_fought.

38. Alfred Edersheim, *The Life and Times of Jesus the Messiah,* vol. 2 (London: Longman's, Green, and Co., 1883), 609, https://books.google.com/books?id=VJUHAAAAQAAJ.

39. Phillips Brooks, "Immortality," sermon 9 in *The Spiritual Man and Other Sermons,* 3rd ed. (London: R. D. Dickson, 1895), 152, emphasis added.

40. Charles H. Spurgeon, *Commentary on Matthew: The Gospel of the Kingdom,* Matthew 27:50, Spurgeon Gems, www.spurgeongems.org/chs_matthew.pdf. Note: This commentary was originally published in 1893 (shortly after Spurgeon's death) under the title *The Gospel of the Kingdom.*

41. Sanders, *Incomparable Christ,* 345.

42. The English word *advent* simply means "arrival" or "coming." Many Christians use the word to refer to the four weeks before Christmas, which traditionally focus not only on Jesus' first arrival on earth as an infant but also His second coming.

More from Nancy DeMoss Wolgemuth

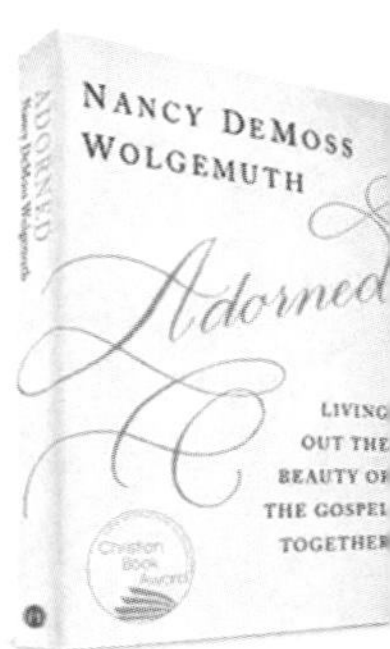

ReviveOurHearts.com